HOW TO BE SUCCESSFULLY PUBLISHED IN MAGAZINES

HOW TO BE SUCCESSFULLY PUBLISHED IN MAGAZINES

The Inside Scoop From Top Editors and Successful Magazine Writers

by Linda Konner

St. Martin's Press
New York

Executive Editor: Toni Lopopolo

Editorial Assistant: Laurie Lindop

Copy Editor: Karen Dubno

Literary Agent: Denise Marcil
                  Denise Marcil Literary Agency

Library of Congress Cataloging-in-Publication Data

How to be successfully published in magazines / [edited by] Linda
    Konner.
        p.   cm.
      ISBN 0-312-04406-2/HC   0-312-04463-1/PB
      1. Authorship—Marketing. I. Konner, Linda.
    PN161.H66 1990
    808'.02—dc20   89-78005

10   9   8   7   6   5   4   3

For Peter, my first Roman

A special thanks to all the editors and writers who agreed to participate in this book.

CONTENTS

Author's Note ix
Introduction xi
1. A Quiz: Should You Be a Freelance Writer? 1
2. How to Catch an Editor's Eye Without Being Obnoxious 7
3. A Quick Course in Editor-Writer Etiquette 11
4. What You Must Know About Every Magazine You Write For 16
5. Nine Ways to Turn Off an Editor 21
6. "What I'm Looking For": Interviews with Magazine Editors 29

 Judith Nolte of *American Baby* 29
 Peter Filichia of *The Best Report* 32
 Andrea Feld of *Bride's* 36
 Susan Gordon of *California* 39
 Kate White of *Child* 42
 Judith Coyne of *Glamour* 46
 Dianne Partie Lange of *Health* 50
 Nelson Aldrich, Jr., of *Lear's* 53
 Anne Summers of *Ms.* 56
 Ellen Sweet of *New Choices for the Best Years* 60
 Larry Smith of *Parade* 63
 Ann Pleshette Murphy of *Parents* 67
 Peter Bloch of *Penthouse* 70
 Patricia Bisesto of *Playgirl* 74
 Susan Lyne and Peter Biskind of *Premiere* 77
 Clell Bryant of *Reader's Digest* 79
 Steven Reddicliffe of *Self* 83
 Roberta Anne Myers of *Seventeen* 86

Mike Schwanz of *Sports Afield* 90
Janel Bladow of *The Star* 93
Duncan Maxwell Anderson of *Success* 97
Pamela Fiori of *Travel & Leisure* 100
Myles Callum of *TV Guide* 103
Susan Shipman of *Vis à Vis* 107
Rosemarie Lennon of *Woman* 110
Sally Koslow of *Woman's Day* 113
Jeanne Muchnick of *Woman's World* 116
Susan Seliger of *Working Mother* 119
7. Successful Magazine Writers and What
  They Do Right 124
    Jennifer Allen 124
    Dan Carlinsky 127
    Sherry Suib Cohen 131
    Mary Alice Kellogg 134
    Vanda Krefft 138
    William Marsano 141
    Sara Nelson 145
    Antonia van der Meer 148
    Ira Wolfman 152
    Dan Yakir 155
8. Sticky Situations—and How to Get Out of
  Them 160
9. Earning a Living from Your Writing 167
10. Final Words 176
Glossary 181

} AUTHOR'S NOTE }

The publishing business being what it is these days, editors come and go at a fairly steady clip. By the time you've had a chance to study this book, some of the people quoted here may have switched jobs. Addresses, phone numbers, and other statistical information at the end of each editor's section may also change.

This doesn't mean, however, that these editors' comments are no longer valid—in some cases it's quite the contrary. For instance, if an editor has attained a *higher* position, her remarks will be all the more significant to you as a potential contributor because her power will be greater. Even in the situation where the editor has gone on to a different magazine, her editorial vision will soon be imposed there. As for the magazine she's left behind, her influence will surely linger on for some time to come.

Therefore, you should use this book as a basis for understanding what editors want, but always stay current by referring to the *most recent* issues of magazines you wish to write for.

INTRODUCTION

A well-regarded author once said about a certain magazine editor-in-chief, "He reminds one what a masochist and jerk you have to be to be a magazine writer."

This may be an ironic way to begin a book on magazine writing, but not an untruthful one. From personal experience I know what that author is talking about. I've been a published magazine writer for nineteen years, and I've endured so many unfortunate experiences during that time that sometimes I wonder why I stay in this business.

Perhaps that's the reason I become exasperated by gung-ho newcomers who don't know what they're getting into, who insist on joining the already swollen ranks of freelance writers. I hear students in my nonfiction workshops say, "I *must* write." "This is what I was *born* to do." "I've wanted to be a magazine writer since I read my first issue of *Highlights for Children*." Maybe; I won't deny another person's passion. But those kinds of remarks cause me at the very least to raise an eyebrow, just as I do when I hear someone exclaim, "I *love* people!" *Please!* Not everyone is lovable, and not everyone who wants to write should try to earn a living as a writer.

Writers, by and large, have a hard life if (1) they're not Tom Wolfe, (2) they're not married to Tom Wolfe, or (3) they're not Tom Wolfe's tailor. That is to say, if you're not already a phenomenally successful writer or being supported by one, you're probably going to have to work hard, constantly come up with new ideas, pound on editors' doors in a humiliating fashion, and not see very much dough for your efforts.

If you like money in large quantities and on a regular basis, freelance writing isn't for you. You'll find yourself complaining a lot to everybody, and when there's no one around, you'll mutter to yourself. You'll start eyeing McDonald's employees jealously. So *what* if their uniforms are goofy, you'll think. At least *they* can count on a steady paycheck. You'll reminisce about how well you used to dress, the nice restaurants you once frequented, the days when your hair was cut in a salon instead of over your bathroom sink.

All this, and I haven't even *mentioned* the subject of rejection, which you as a freelance magazine writer will face with staggering regularity. Even when things look like they're perking up for you—you've sold one, maybe two, articles in a month, say—you'll then endure remarkably long periods when editors (and their accounting departments) tell you that you don't have the right stuff or, worse, ignore you altogether. If you don't have a loving mate, an affectionate pup, or a totally unrelated hobby like woodworking to take your mind off your troubles, you'll find it difficult to keep going back to the computer day after day.

But let's just say you refuse to let those things get you

down, that you're the sort of man or woman who doesn't know the meaning of the word *quit*. There are two things you absolutely need to make it as a magazine writer: *talent* and *interpersonal smarts*.

The first—talent—is something I can't help you with, I'm afraid. No, it isn't a case of you either have it or you don't. Even if you *don't* have it, I believe you can *get* it by doing everything in your power to improve your skills: reading more, writing more, taking a writing course or two, joining a writers' workshop where people are *getting published,* not just shmoozing. As with anything else in your life, you'll work on polishing your writing technique to the extent you decide it's important to you. And the nice thing is, you can *always* get better.

I'm here, along with more than three dozen other magazine professionals, to help you with the second item: interpersonal smarts. The premise of *How to Be Successfully Published in Magazines* is that there's far more to being a successful writer than possessing writing ability. There's also the seldom-defined area of interpersonal skills, that combination of personality traits and professionalism that makes you a pleasure—or a pain—to work with from an editor's point of view. You may have impressive writing credentials and still get the runaround at a publication. While it may not be your breath, it could be your obnoxious telephone manner or your know-it-all attitude or your reluctance to follow directions. *How to Be Successfully Published in Magazines* is filled with guidelines culled from my own experiences as a magazine editor and freelance writer and from those of the magazine editors and writers I interviewed. Covered are such nitty-gritty topics as, among others, how to capture an editor's attention, the rules of editor-writer etiquette, and how to get out of sticky situations with an editor—tips that may motivate you to change your ways, to the benefit of your writing.

The twenty-eight magazine editors quoted here describe in detail and at length the recent features they've bought, what makes them so special, and—most importantly—what constitutes a good editor-writer relationship. They provide candid answers to such crucial and rarely asked questions as:

- What do your favorite writers do right?
- What turns you off about people in general and freelance writers in particular?
- If your best friend approached you about writing for your magazine, what advice would you give?
- Have you ever stopped working with a writer without giving an explanation, and why?
- What are the "secrets" of making a sale to your magazine?
- What would induce you to invite a writer out to lunch?
- Which recently purchased stories have been your favorites, and why?

In addition, you'll find specific, anecdote-packed statements from ten of the country's most successful freelance writers, who reveal insights they've picked up along the way and tips on turning a life's passion—magazine journalism—into a full-fledged and lucrative career.

In this way *How to Be Successfully Published in Magazines* transcends the usual how-to-write guides and more closely resembles books like *What They Don't Teach You at Harvard Business School,* brimming with subtle hints for success based to a large degree on person-to-person interactions.

After interviewing the editors and writers quoted here— and later, while transcribing and editing their wise, funny, and heartfelt comments—I came to understand and appreciate my chosen career in a way I never had before. Even after having freelanced for nineteen years and been an editor for thirteen, I was now privy to fresh insights from men and women whose years in the magazine business amounted to *centuries* of experience.

I didn't scoff when Sherry Suib Cohen told me that living the life of a freelance writer was a dream come true, yet I also saw why writer Dan Carlinsky believes you have to be nuts to get into the business. I could relate to editors Larry Smith and Susan Seliger, who had done their time as at-home writers and were now contentedly back in an office. Yet I couldn't help but detect a *twinge* of jealousy when certain editors spoke about the freelance writers they knew.

As for me, I see far more cons than pros to this lifestyle, so I've never knowingly encouraged any but the most determined, disciplined writers to embark on a freelancing career. And yet . . . being a writer has given me a wonderful life I would never have had any other way. Magazine writing has enabled me to cover the World Monopoly Championship in Monte Carlo, dance with the Bora Indians in a Peruvian hut, sail on luxury liners, attend a Weight Watchers class in Hong Kong, meet the Vice President of Costa Rica, have coffee with Kirk Douglas, spend a weekend in the same Detroit hotel suite former President Reagan stayed in the weekend before, taste barbecued rattlesnake in Colorado, appear on national TV, explore a New Zealand snail ranch, visit Cher at home—*and* get paid for it all, no less. Because I think travel and show business are the most exciting and fun-packed subjects, I've made them my writing specialties, but I know that *any* area of interest to me can be an excuse for a story—and an adventure.

This is why I'm a writer.

I don't earn all the money in the world, my possessions are modest, I don't have a husband or children, and yet I feel very lucky to live the life I do. I don't know if I'm the envy of millions, but I often think I should be.

HOW TO BE SUCCESSFULLY PUBLISHED IN MAGAZINES

A QUIZ:
SHOULD YOU BE
A FREELANCE WRITER?

You may think you should be a writer. Maybe even your spouse, mother, and extension-course writing instructor think you should be a writer. But as we all know it's one thing to *write* and another thing to regard it as a potential *career*.

You may or may not have a suitable temperament for such a lifestyle. And you might not have the staying power crucial to getting your career off the ground—and keeping it aloft.

This quiz will answer some of your questions about the nature of the business and your ability to survive as a freelancer.

. . . .

1. Do people always tell you what a fascinating storyteller you are?
Yes _____ No _____

2. Are you a good listener, one who generally finds other people and what they say interesting?
Yes _____ No _____

3. When someone else tells a story, do you find yourself asking a lot of questions?
Yes _____ No _____

4. Are you a good mimic?
Yes _____ No _____

5. Do you often watch a TV show or read a magazine ad and believe you could have written it better?
Yes _____ No _____

6. Have you ever come up with an original idea for a creating a new magazine?
Yes _____ No _____

7. Do you find yourself jotting down ideas and notes on cocktail napkins and scraps of paper?
Yes _____ No _____

8. Have you ever done something really outrageous just to see what would happen?
Yes _____ No _____

9. Have you ever come up with an invention?
Yes _____ No _____

10. Did you go as far as to have it patented or developed?
Yes _____ No _____

11. If someone offered you an all-expenses-paid trip to the moon, would you take it?
Yes _____ No _____

12. Do you read just about anything you can get your hands on?
Yes _____ No _____

13. Do you hate to be alone?
Yes _____ No _____

14. Do you keep diaries and write wonderful letters?
Yes _____ No _____

15. Do you want to be a writer so you can be famous and respected?
Yes _____ No _____

16. So you can be rich?
Yes _____ No _____

17. Because you have so much to say you can't help writing it all down?
Yes _____ No _____

18. If you had one extra hour every day, how would you spend it?
Sleeping _____ Cleaning _____ Writing _____ Watching TV _____

19. Has writing given you greater insight into yourself and other people?
Yes _____ No _____

20. Did you bother to do this quiz?
Yes _____ No _____

ANSWERS

1. YES. Good talkers tend to be good writers—*if* they take the time to get their words down on paper. These days many books are "written" with a tape recorder, such as Kirk Douglas's best-selling autobiography, *The Ragman's Son.*

2. YES. Good listeners make good writers, enabling them to accumulate story ideas, pick up nuances of speech and personality, and learn empathy.

3. YES. Details are what make one's writing come alive, and you can easily gather them from everyday conversations. You also need a basic curiosity about others to be a writer.

4. YES. If you can successfully imitate others, you'll be able to create vivid characters in your writing.

5. YES. Writers constantly think, *I* could do that—or better! *Successful* writers act upon their belief and *produce.*

6. YES. Successful freelance writers so immerse themselves in article ideas for existing magazines that, sooner or later, they think up a concept for a magazine that's fresh and original.

7. YES. Successful writers can't seem to turn off the ideas, no matter where they are. Because they know that ideas are fleeting, they're smart enough to write them down.

8. YES. A writer will do almost anything to satisfy that "What if. . . ?" curiosity.

9. YES. A vivid imagination is a necessity for a writer.

10. YES. It's not enough to dream; you must also *act.*

11. YES. The best writers tend to be the most adventurous people.

12. YES. The more you read, the better your own writing inevitably becomes.

13. NO. Writing is a solitary profession. No matter how many meetings with editors you have or how many interviews you conduct, you'll be by yourself more often than not. If that's not your idea of fun, try something else.

14. YES. Don't dismiss excellent writing even if it's read only by you and your brother overseas. Good writing is good writing. *Now* what are you going to do with it?

15. YES. Worthy goals. If you don't aspire to greatness, why bother?

16. YES. Ditto. Shoot for the stars, but be realistic, too.

17. YES. Okay, but you also need talent and direction.

18. WRITING. Sure, snoozing and "L.A. Law" are more relaxing, but they won't help your career. (If you'd rather *clean* than write, try another occupation.)

19. YES. Writing creates a lovely cycle: it brings greater understanding of the human condition, which, in turn, enhances one's writing.

20. YES. If not, how serious can you possibly be?

SCORING

15–20 correct answers: Good! Now get to that word processor.

1–14 correct answers: Are you *sure* you want to be a magazine writer? Try freelancing part-time for six months, then take this quiz again to see if you can improve your score. But whatever you do, don't give up your day job!

. . . .

{ 2 }

HOW TO CATCH AN EDITOR'S EYE
Without Being Obnoxious

Are you serious about working your way out of the slush pile and into an editor's stable of regular contributors? These suggestions will help.

1. LEARN HOW TO COMPOSE THE DYNAMITE QUERY LETTER

There's no getting around it: if an editor doesn't know you personally, your only hope is to sell yourself with your top-notch ideas and your writing ability. The quickest way to show what you've got is by composing a query (or pitch letter) that will knock his or her Reeboks off.

If you think your queries need work, there are plenty of good books out there that will show you how to give your letters the punch they lack. For now, though, here's a quick troubleshooter's checklist:

- Does your letter look flawless, with every word spelled right?
- Is your query one page only? (If you *can't* confine your thoughts to a single page, you haven't sufficiently extracted the essence of the idea.)
- Do you limit yourself to one or two ideas?
- Does your query start out as intriguingly as your article would? Or have you opened with the horrifyingly dull "I would like to write an article about. . ."?
- Is your idea specific enough? Have you successfully conveyed why your idea is perfect for this particular publication?
- Did you include a (verified) statistic or quote that indicates you've done some preliminary research?
- If the idea is for a particular section or column of the magazine, do you mention that section by name?
- Did you assign your idea a working title that's good enough to be used on the cover?
- Have you made sure your idea has not appeared in the last six issues (at least) of the magazine you're querying?
- Do you (briefly) mention your credentials at the end?
- Have you enclosed one or two (not more) impressive clips of your work? (If you've only managed thus far to get published in the Letters to the Editor column or the Hoboken *Pennysaver*, forget the clips.)

2. BE PERSISTENT

You lose your momentum with a magazine when you send one or two queries that get turned down and then you disappear. Especially if you've gotten close-but-no-cigar-type replies from an editor, you should keep going, keep submitting ideas. Your name will stay in the editor's mind, and if you're essentially on the right track, you'll get an assignment sooner or later.

3. GO WHERE EDITORS CONGREGATE

If you can meet editors outside the office and you make a favorable impression, you have a better chance of landing an assignment than if you remain a faceless query-sender. Join a writers' organization such as the American Society of Journalists and Authors or the National Writers Union. Magazine editors are frequently called upon to be guest speakers, and you can meet them during the cocktail hour or impress them during the discussion session. Attend meetings of writers and editors at your local library. Talk to editors at writing classes or writers' conferences (but don't monopolize their time). Whether you've heard an editor speak at a conference or had the opportunity to chat with one, always follow up with a query the next day, making a flattering reference to his or her talk.

4. EXPLOIT YOUR EXISTING CONTACTS

It isn't just "who you know" when it comes to career success, but making the most of your network of friends and acquaintances in the business will lead to better relationships with editors. If your pals don't mind your approaching their editors and dropping their names, do so—but *only* after you've established that they have a sound working relationship. (If your friend's last two stories were killed by the editor you're courting, you *don't* want to use that name.) Find out from writer buddies who's in and who's out at the magazines you hope to write for, what sort of articles they're looking for these days, and what the pay scale is. And, of course, return the favor by mentioning sales you've recently made, areas of expertise your pal may be able to exploit at publications you know well, and good old-fashioned gossip.

Offer a friend's name to an editor who is looking for a writer whose specialty is something other than yours. And, as one editor points out in this book, freelancers are often in the best position to hear about staff jobs. If you know your editor is unhappy and would appreciate being told about an opening at another publication, mention it. (Make sure it's a *great* job, though.) Whether or not your editor ultimately gets it, he or she will be grateful for your concern.

A QUICK COURSE IN
EDITOR-WRITER ETIQUETTE

Ah, editors . . . some writers think editors are a species unto themselves. Actually, they're really not much different from you and me, except they tend to wear nicer jewelry, take longer lunch hours, and not answer their own phone. But they crave the same things in life the rest of us want: a house in the country, a loving mate, and as little on-the-job irritation as possible.

How do you do *your* part? Are you going to be that writer who makes magazine editors wish they were never born? Or will they greet *your* midafternoon call like the arrival of an unexpected royalty check?

Just as there is a certain etiquette that civilized people follow when being introduced to the Queen or attending a bar mitzvah, there is an etiquette in dealing with magazine editors. Follow it closely—and watch your career take off.

1. IF YOU'RE A COMPLETE UNKNOWN TO AN EDITOR, WRITE FIRST

No editor—no *person*—likes to pick up the telephone and hear, "You don't know me, but . . ." It almost doesn't matter what follows that opening: the editor is automatically going to tune out and mentally be cursing the secretary for not answering the phone or for putting your call through. Your credentials could be great, you might have a terrific article idea, and you might ultimately get seven assignments from this editor. But *right now* this editor doesn't want to know you.

A better approach: Drop a note to the editor and include one or two (not more) of your most impressive clips. Have a great, on-target idea that's perfect for the magazine. Indicate you will call within the week. Call. The reception you get will be much warmer, I guarantee.

You *may* call, however, if you and the editor have already met somewhere—a luncheon, a writers' conference—or if a mutual friend or colleague suggested you do so. Even then, keep it brief—introduce yourself, make your point, and hang up.

2. CHARM THE EDITOR BY CHARMING THE ASSISTANT

It pays to be nice to everyone in life, but it especially pays with assistants to the editors for whom you want to write. Treat secretaries like slaves and you can be sure they'll give you comparable service; treat them like equals and you'll be amazed how well their bosses wind up treating *you*.

This isn't to say there aren't a lot of bad secretaries out there who are frustrating to deal with; of course there are.

But it's smart to give them the benefit of the doubt. I always cringe whenever I overhear someone mistreat a secretary solely on the basis of his or her *status*. The writer who does this is invariably the type who pours on the (fake) charm with the editor or boss.

I have a different method. When dealing with a secretary or rock-bottom editorial assistant, I immediately begin by mentally elevating that person from the actual job. For instance, I never ask if the person answering the phone is So-and-So's secretary. Instead I ask, "Do you work with [not *for*] So-and-So?" I treat the person with respect and with the attitude that I'd really like his or her help. Then, if we've been talking for more than a sentence or two, I'll ask the assistant's name so I can start getting into the habit of using it in future conversations. Needless to say, the call is liberally sprinkled with "please" and "thank you."

If you've never behaved this way with a secretary or editorial assistant (someone who, by the way, may be your *next* editor six months from now), try it—you'll be astounded how well it works. Manipulation? Some might say so. But if that's what it is, you can manipulate me any time.

3. LAND THE IN-PERSON MEETING

If you and your editor are in the same city, you might be eager to set up a meeting after having dealt exclusively by phone or by mail for months. Once it becomes clear that the two of you have something of a future together— you've sold the magazine a few stories and there have been no major hassles—you won't be out of line to suggest an in-person meeting if the editor hasn't already done so.

Try something casual like, "I'm going to be in the neighborhood tomorrow afternoon. Will you be available for five or ten minutes? My article is done, and I'd love to drop it off and say hello in person." It's hard for an editor who essentially likes you to refuse such a request. And a successful person-to-person meeting—even a very brief one—tends to lead to a better working relationship.

Once you're there, do as you promised: keep it brief unless *the editor* makes it clear that you should stick around a bit longer.

4. ONCE YOU BECOME A REGULAR, KEEP YOUR EDITOR APPRISED OF ANY CHANGE IN YOUR SCHEDULE

If you've been getting steady assignments from a magazine, be sure to tell your editor if you're going on vacation for two weeks or if some other personal or professional matter will keep you from doing work for her. The sooner you can let the editor know, the better.

And never, never disappear without a word when you know your presence may be crucial, such as right after your article has been accepted and it's ready to be edited and fact-checked.

5. BECOME INDISPENSABLE TO YOUR EDITOR

This may not sound as though it should fall under the heading of "etiquette," but it will to your editor. It's much of what you've heard time and time again, but the information never loses its value. Be pleasant in your dealings with the editor. Keep your calls brief and to the point. Meet all your deadlines, especially when you know he or she needs something in a pinch. Go the extra mile—give the editor a bit more than what was hoped for. Make sure your writing is up to par and the information is accurate. Let the editor know you're available for future assignments.

You'll have no shortage of work from that editor—or any other.

{ 4 }

WHAT YOU MUST KNOW
ABOUT EVERY MAGAZINE
YOU WRITE FOR

You're in your dentist's office, and you flip through a new magazine that you think you'd like to write for. You may even have what you consider the perfect idea for it. Fine—but you have miles to go before you can put pencil to paper (or fingers to computer keyboard). At this point you know virtually nothing about the magazine in question, and you've got to be a lot more informed about it before you can compose a query that an editor can take seriously.

There are certain basics a freelancer must know about all publications. These basics involve learning to "read" a magazine on several levels.

1. THE TITLE

Every magazine has a title, of course, and its aim is to give the potential buyer of the publication a fairly good idea of the content and style within. Some titles are pretty straightforward. Others can be misleading. If you haven't thoroughly examined one or two issues of a magazine and properly figured out its target audience—or if you've simply spotted a magazine title in a directory without exploring further—it might prove embarrassing for you.

For example, a friend of mine used to be an editor at *Circus*, a rock 'n' roll publication. After he got his fifth or sixth query letter suggesting a profile of Emmett Kelly, he lost his patience. Another editor pal told me that a freelancer actually asked him whether his magazine, formerly called *50 Plus*, was one that featured, as he put it, "chesty girls." (And, no, *Facets* magazine is *not* for plumbers, and *Snoopy* is *not* the house organ of the Central Intelligence Agency.)

Because titles can be misleading, you'll have to go beyond the magazine's name. Which leads to . . .

2. COVER PHOTOS AND COVERLINES

Examining cover photos will clear up a lot of confusion. So will reading coverlines, those eye-catching words and phrases running over the model's hair and along the sides of her face or body. These represent the blockbuster stories in the issue, the ones the editors think will sell the magazine. The day your story makes it as a coverline is the day you've automatically increased your value to that publication. When you come up with an article idea, think in terms of whether or not it will play as a coverline—in fact, always try to give your article a title that can be coverlined.

3. THE MASTHEAD

The list near the front of the magazine of all the editors' titles and names (*always* spelled correctly here) is the masthead. The most current address and phone number of the magazine also will usually appear at the bottom of the masthead or at the bottom of a nearby page. Figure out from the masthead who would be the likeliest person to receive your query—generally someone with a title like articles editor or senior editor or features editor—and you'll save the time it takes to reroute your letter if you addressed it to the editor-in-chief.

4. FREELANCE VERSUS STAFF-WRITTEN STORIES

It's amazing how often freelance writers will suggest topics for magazine columns that are *not* open to freelance material. You will avoid making this mistake by comparing the name on the column with the names on the masthead—regular columnists generally win the title contributing editor—and reading several issues of the magazine to see if that person's name *always* appears on that particular column. If it does, stay away. However, many magazine columns *do* seek freelance pieces; just learn to distinguish these from the category described above. And, of course, most feature articles are written by freelancers.

5. READ MANY ISSUES OF A MAGAZINE, INCLUDING THE CURRENT ONE

If you think you know a magazine by reading one or two issues, think again. Most editors recommend that you carefully study at least a half-dozen. The point is, *you'll* know when you get the hang of a particular publication, its style and its readers. And *always* look at the most recent issue of any magazine before submitting a query to make sure the personnel or the address or both haven't changed. Although *Writer's Market* is a wonderful sourcebook, this is one time *not* to trust its information.

6. MANUSCRIPT LENGTH

If you think your story will require 2,500 words, don't plan on submitting it for a section of the magazine that only runs 1,000-word pieces. Editors hate getting manuscripts that are thousands of words longer (or shorter) than the expected length.

7. LEAD TIMES

Most monthly magazines have lead times of from three to six months; weeklies have lead times of anywhere from one to ten weeks. If you're dealing with holiday and seasonal material, you must allow even more time because these issues are usually planned very far in advance. To be absolutely sure of the magazine's lead time, call and ask.

8. MULTIPLE SUBMISSIONS

The rule of multiple submissions—that is, don't submit your idea to more than one editor at a time—works in favor of the editor and not the writer. It forces the writer to wait, sometimes months, for each individual editor to make up his or her mind about a story idea. I used to urge writers to strictly obey the multiple submissions rule. Now my feeling is that it's no sin to send the same idea off to two magazines as long as you're prepared for the consequences: both editors may give you the assignment, and the one you sheepishly turn down isn't going to be too thrilled with you. However, the possibility of *that* happening is slim enough to take the chance, I think. After all, your livelihood depends directly on how many stories you write and sell, while an editor will continue to pick up his or her paycheck no matter how long it takes to make a decision on a query.

9. PAYMENT RATES AND RIGHTS

Does the publication you're interested in pay ten cents a word, two dollars a word, or only in copies of the magazine? Does it pay upon acceptance (processing of payment begins when you're told the story's been bought) or upon publication (which might mean you may never see a dime)? Does the magazine purchase first or one-time rights, or all rights (which means you cannot resell your story)? The answers to these questions can be found in the most current volume of *Writer's Market,* an indispensable handbook for freelancers. Otherwise, be sure to ask your editor *before* accepting any assignment.

{ 5 }

NINE WAYS TO
TURN OFF AN EDITOR

I've been told I'm a pretty happy-go-lucky person most of the time, and that as an editor I'm unusually accessible to and supportive of writers. But even the cheeriest of us can occasionally get discouraged by what writers do in the name of making a sale.

I've worked with freelancers for five years at *Seventeen* magazine, four at *Weight Watchers Magazine,* four at *Woman's World,* and one at *Redbook,* and the unprofessional sights and sounds coming from some of them are mind-boggling. But I've discovered that when you give people enough negative examples, they eventually learn the right thing to do.

Here, then, are nine of my writers' favorite ways to torment me. (And as you'll see from the interviews that follow, other editors are similarly tormented.) I offer these examples to you in the hope that, if you're guilty of any, you'll recognize yourself—and stop immediately.

TURNOFF NO. 1: SPELL MY NAME WRONG

Misspelling a name may seem like a minor point, but not to an editor. Many of them are pretty big egomaniacs. I, for one, am dismayed to see my name spelled *Conner* or *Konnor* or *O'Connor* or even *Lynda*. When you realize that my name appears on the masthead of every issue of *Woman's World* magazine, it's hard to fathom how someone can get it wrong. (And when a writer starts off a query to me with "Dear Sir," there's trouble ahead!)

My feelings about misspelling my name also apply to other spelling errors and typos in the rest of the query or manuscript. To me, they're obvious signs of a writer's carelessness. If a writer is careless here, we editors think, how careful will he or she be about the facts and quotes in the article?

TURNOFF NO. 2: USE STATIONERY THAT SCREAMS "AMATEUR!"

Like most editors I've spoken to, I think I've seen it all when it comes to the writing paper used for the queries I've received: floral stationery, pink pussycats in the corner, even scented paper. I don't know . . . maybe these free-lancers think they're writing to *Romantic Times*.

Just as bad is using stationery with a drawing of a type-writer (old-fashioned) or a word processor (newer but not better), or the words "Freelance Writer" printed under the writer's name. When I get what *looks* like a query letter, I *assume* I'm dealing with a freelance writer. Those labels or cute little symbols on someone's stationery only tell me that the writer is not quite convinced of that status.

I also know writers who've had all their credentials printed on their stationery, usually crammed in along the bottom or the sides. One freelancer even went as far as to surprint lightly on the paper miniature logos of the magazines she'd written for. Not only did that make her queries difficult to read, but I was not even impressed by the publications highlighted. (Anyway, if the editor is unfamiliar with your work, simply include that information in the last paragraph of your query.)

The best paper to use is plain white or off-white bond, printed only with your name, address, and phone number.

TURNOFF NO. 3: CALL ME—EVEN THOUGH YOU DON'T KNOW ME

Yes, a phone call is quicker and easier than a letter—but for *whom*? Not only does the average editor hate being interrupted during a hectic day by an unfamiliar (and usually long-winded) voice on the telephone, but it's difficult to adequately evaluate the merits of your suggestion that way. (Chances are the editor you're calling isn't the final arbiter of an idea anyway; he or she will usually have to discuss it with one or more bosses.) Ultimately you're the one who loses out. Another telephone tip: Few things drive an editor crazier than when a writer calls with an idea that's rejected and quickly adds, "That's okay; I can think of some more ideas!"

So don't call an editor you don't know to pitch a story. There are only two exceptions to this rule: (1) when you've already sold your work to another editor at that publication, a point you should bring up within the first ten seconds of the conversation; and (2) when the story idea is so hot and so timely and so perfect for that particular magazine that sending a query letter would simply take too long.

(But you'd better be *very* sure that your idea meets those criteria.)

And if you're phoning long-distance, *never* call an unknown editor collect!

TURNOFF NO. 4: BECOME TOO FAMILIAR WITH ME

Over the years I've developed an excellent working relationship with many of my writers, ones I actually look forward to hearing from on the phone. Yet there are those freelancers who mistakenly believe that once they've made a sale or two to me, they have license to get real chummy.

There's one writer, for instance, who calls me "Sweetie" and "Hon," and another who refers to me as "Darlin'." I hate terms of endearment except from those who've endeared themselves to me in my personal life. I don't have the heart to clue in these writers because their crime is relatively harmless, although I suspect they're similarly clueless about other areas of their lives.

Then there are those writers who want me to know about *them*. They explain, for example, that they're pitching me a story on animal rights because they've campaigned against vivisection every summer since 1977. That's all *very* interesting, I assure them, but I really prefer that they get to the point. (And after a while, if they *can't* get to the point, I'm going to start being too busy to take their calls.)

Editors give off plenty of signals with their tone of voice. Learn to read these signals, especially if they say, "Stick to business."

TURNOFF NO. 5: EXAGGERATE THE VALUE OF YOUR IDEA (OR YOURSELF)

I realize that freelance writers are, as a group, an under-appreciated lot. Busy editors don't praise them nearly as much as they should for their good suggestions, skillful writing, and overall dependability. During those weeks when the rejection slips seem to be piling up more quickly than usual, it's easy for a writer to feel unloved by the publishing world. Often the freelancer will compensate by getting carried away by an idea that truly excites him or her or by a piece he or she is eager to write.

Yet it's important to curb your impulse to boast to an editor about how perfect an idea is for that magazine and how you're the only person who can do the topic justice. "I've got a terrific idea . . ." is a phrase that has introduced many snoozy ones, or ones that simply aren't right for a specific publication. Just present the facts, and let the editor be the judge of their merit. Furthermore, if an idea should be turned down for whatever reason, *don't* debate that decision. Trust that the editor knows the magazine's editorial needs better than you do. Chances are slim that you'll succeed in changing his or her mind.

TURNOFF NO. 6: MISS DEADLINES

At most of the magazines where I've worked, I've given my writers deadlines for completing their articles. I find that setting deadlines makes record keeping easier for me as well as helps writers who have a tendency to procrastinate.

Editors like to know that writers can be relied upon to get manuscripts in on time, especially when they've been scheduled for a particular issue. When writers routinely fail to meet their deadlines, editors aren't happy—and aren't apt to give them future assignments. On the other hand, if you prove that you're someone an editor can count on, chances are good you'll be thought of when something is needed in a pinch. So take your deadlines seriously.

Often, though, deadlines—and editors—are flexible. If you *must* have an extension—because the person you're set to interview postponed the meeting, for example, or because a close relative died—then give your editor a quick call to explain the situation and ask for more time. You'll probably get it.

TURNOFF NO. 7: SHOW YOUR IGNORANCE

Your shortcomings will emerge soon enough without your hurrying things along. There's absolutely nothing to be gained—and much to be lost—if you flaunt your ignorance of a publication and its policies (or your *own* ignorance).

So if your idea has been turned down by Magazine A and you're now submitting it to Magazine B, do *not* say something like, "Magazine A rejected it, but I think it would still be perfect for you." Who asked you? No editor wants to get some other editor's castoffs, even though it happens all the time.

Don't volunteer any potentially harmful information. And *don't* make statements about a magazine to its editor unless you're certain of your facts. For example, when a writer calls me at *Woman's World* and says, "I know you don't do stories about male celebrities . . ." (we *do*), it drives me wild—especially when the current issue carries a photo and coverline about a Bruce Springsteen feature.

26

TURNOFF NO. 8: SEND PHOTOCOPIED OR MESSY MANUSCRIPTS

An editor who receives a photocopied or ratty-looking manuscript feels just as crummy as the editor who has been told another magazine rejected the idea he or she is now considering. They both know the writer has unsuccessfully been trying to seduce other editors into buying the same article.

Every editor wants to be treated as special and longs to believe your submission was meant for him or her alone. Therefore, unless a magazine specifies otherwise (in directories like *Writer's Market*), only send originals. And if your manuscript doesn't come back to you dewy fresh, do up another one. (This is the perfect argument for using a word processor, capable of printing up spanking new copies in minutes.) Which brings us to . . .

TURNOFF NO. 9: USE A TYPEWRITER

This may sound surprising and rather bold, particularly coming from someone who was a long-time technophobe. However, I believe you can often separate the pros from the amateurs by the equipment they use, and a computer-generated query or manuscript tells me a writer takes herself and her work seriously.

These days there's almost no excuse for even a part-time writer not to own a computer. Anyone who expects to make at least a few thousand dollars a year from freelance writing can afford to invest in a basic word-processing system, which can be had for under $1500. It's relatively easy to learn how to use a word processor, and the expense will be recouped after a few magazine sales. The increased ease and productivity make a computer a necessity to anyone who claims to be a writer. As one seven-year computer veteran and successful freelancer puts it, "Going back to a typewriter now would be a death sentence."

In this day and age, a writer who continues to use a typewriter—with all its attendant hassles for both writer (endless retyping) and editor (less-than-perfect copies)—is making life needlessly difficult.

{ 6 }

"WHAT I'M LOOKING FOR": INTERVIEWS WITH MAGAZINE EDITORS

JUDITH NOLTE, EDITOR, *AMERICAN BABY*

"Skip the shmoozing. Make it clean and neat and easy and fast."

"There are a couple of things that bother me about writers. The first—not to mention the second, third, fourth, and fifth—is when they telephone me. Generally they call about a problem—such as why I didn't like their last article—but I choose not to answer that kind of question on their nickel. That's a call *I* want to make; let *me* take the initiative. The writer may be asking for answers I can't give on the spot, like 'How can I make the piece better?' They look to me almost like a teacher (which in fact I once was), but frankly I don't want to work with a writer that way. I

29

feel a professional writer should *know* how to make her story good.

"I think much of my attitude has to do with the type of magazine *American Baby* is. Perhaps if I were the editor of a publication with a strong literary tradition, I'd feel differently—I'd know the writing itself is paramount and that getting the pieces I wanted might require more massaging of the words, more discussion with the writer. But that's just not the case at *American Baby,* where our goal is to provide useful information, clearly and concisely. I don't enjoy spending a lot of time working closely with writers— I just want the words in front of me, in a completed manuscript, for me to tinker with.

"I'm looking for decently written pieces based on deeply felt issues—and I believe that if you don't feel deeply about the subject of parenting and baby care, you can't put it across very well. *American Baby* is a hands-on service magazine, aimed at women in the late stages of their pregnancy through the birth and first couple of years of their babies' lives. It's a mixture of medical, behavioral, and practical stories, including solid product and service information. The tone of the magazine is, above all, supportive. We offer pregnant women and new mothers a support system, telling them, in effect, that they're not alone, that although this is a confusing and often difficult time, they'll get through it.

"I depend tremendously on freelance writers for our stories. We spend a lot of time reading our mail, and we uncover some very good writers with fresh ideas that way. But I've also found, regrettably, that the lifespan of the average *American Baby* writer is relatively short. Our writers are frequently women (and men) who've been profoundly inspired by their own recent parenthood experiences, but once their own infants start to grow up, they lose some of their interest in writing about small babies.

"Like other editors, I'm always looking for a new twist. As you can imagine, we constantly recycle subjects, and we even reprint our own articles from time to time. So when a writer comes up with a fresh take on a tried-and-true topic, I'm delighted. For example, one woman recently wrote to us about how, when she realized she couldn't afford child care, she started a day-care center in her home for her child and a half-dozen others. Her subsequent article—what to look for when choosing a day-care facility—was terrific because she provided relevant anecdotes from both sides of the fence, as a mother *and* as a child-care provider.

"I don't have more than a couple of writers whom I use over and over again, writers who give me exactly what I'm looking for or more. One is a writer who is also a childbirth educator. She first queried us about a story on episiotomy, and she did a wonderful job. Now she's doing another piece on caesareans. She knows her subject well and can write colorfully, even about fairly technical matters. My other favorite writer is a man who's the father of three. Not only does he have a smooth, easy writing style, but he's also a pleasure to deal with. He comes up to the office to deliver his manuscript—on time—and he'll sit politely in the waiting room, never insisting on going into an editor's office. I'd love to find a few others like him.

"The best piece of advice I can offer on how to break into *American Baby* is to have—or adopt—a mindset like that of our readers. If a writer displays the kind of sensitivity toward her subject matter that a mother would display to her newborn, she's on the right track. I need to be able to see from your query that you can talk to a parent without being preachy. It helps if you're a parent yourself, but if you aren't, you should still be able to offer that warm, soft shoulder to the reader, even when discussing a difficult subject like C-sections or amniocentesis. Remember, the person reading *American Baby* is excited, frightened, intensely interested in her baby, and in need of a lot of encouragement. She's concerned about her child and about whether she's doing the right thing. If you, as a writer, can answer a reader's concerns and sound reassuring without being a know-it-all, you'll do well.

"In short, I'm always looking for good writers, but I hate being badgered by them. So skip the shmoozing. Make it clean and neat and easy and fast. Simply send me a one-page query, with one or two ideas, not five. When you write your story, deliver what—and when—you promise. And learn how to take a blow every now and then. Do that and I guarantee you good results at *American Baby*."

AMERICAN BABY, 475 Park Avenue South, New York, NY 10017; (212) 689-3600.
Frequency of Publication: monthly.
Circulation: 1.1 million, 90 percent controlled circulation (free to new and expectant parents and doctors).
Readership: primarily pregnant women and the mothers of infants.
Available Upon Request: free writer's guidelines and sample copy.
Payment Rate: first article on speculation, thirty cents a word thereafter.

PETER FILICHIA, EDITOR, *THE BEST REPORT*

"I will never use a writer who tries to pull a fast one."

"*The Best Report* is a nine-year-old magazine whose subtitle is *Exploring the World of Quality.* Our 100,000 monthly readers are mainly male professionals with annual incomes over $100,000—and much of it is money to burn. *The Best Report* is filled with articles on price-is-no-object accessories, hobbies, gadgets, luxury travel, handcrafted items, personal services, and grown-up, rich-man toys. The style is serious, yet not deadly so. Stories for *The Best Report* should be written with an admiring, what-will-they-think-of-next attitude. Our readers are truly interested in knowing where they can get a pair of hand-tooled ostrich-skin boots for $950 or how to hire a proper English butler. We want to show our readers how to have good times, ways to enjoy their life to the fullest. Thus, Socialist freelance writers who believe such concerns are frivolous and are apt to assume a mocking tone need not apply.

"A typical issue of the magazine includes articles on high-priced reproductions of art deco sculpture, an etiquette class for children, a foldable kayak, the ready-to-wear line of evening gowns created by the Duchess of York's favorite designer, the best restaurants in St. Louis, and ingredients one can purchase to duplicate the Bellinis served at Harry's Bar in Venice.

"Like every editor, I prefer writers who really know our style, who tie in with what we do and why we do it. I'm more than happy to send sample copies of the magazine to writers; they don't request copies nearly as often as they should. In some cases, writers *do* ask me for them, but it's more to show me they're on the ball than anything else. I don't think they really read them, which is discouraging to me as an editor, but it's true, I'm afraid.

"What I like most about writers is when they actually answer the questions they pose in their articles. For instance, one writer did a story on how to buy a franchise in the Major Indoor Lacrosse League—a good topic for us. He mentioned that the league didn't play regular lacrosse but, rather, something called box lacrosse, yet he never bothered to explain the differences between the two games.

It was then up to me to call him and ask about them—and that was a call I should never have had to make. It had been the third article from that writer where crucial information was omitted. I'll never use him again.

"And I will never use a writer who tries to pull a fast one. For instance, we don't buy travel articles—they're all written in-house—but they're the ones offered to us the most because writers like to travel (often for free, via press junkets). I understand that, but it doesn't change our policy. Yet after I explained this to one writer on the phone, she tried to sell me a rose by another name. She insisted, 'I'm not talking about a *travel* piece. It's about a place in Italy where they make the best olive oil.' She was very aggressive—I pictured smoke coming out of her nostrils as she spoke. Not only was her idea a thinly disguised travel article, but if she had read *The Best Report,* she'd have known we recently did a story on olive oil.

"Right now we have a terrific piece in the works, what I call a quintessential *Best Report* story—and it was suggested by a freelancer. It's about Robert Cheroske and Associates, a California real-estate-cum-decorating firm that sells exquisitely decorated homes, completely equipped with state-of-the-art gadgetry. The company's clients include Burt Reynolds and Tom Jones. (By the way, if you can drop celebrity names in your *Best Report* stories, so much the better.) Each home is different. One, for example, might come with a Hers master bathroom equipped with a marble Jacuzzi, an outdoor massage table, a tanning bed, and a dressing room with an electronically controlled conveyor belt; and a His master bath housed inside a two-story glass tower, with a full gym, a big-screen TV, stainless-steel-and-chrome cabinets, and a writing desk. Some homes even come with a Rolls-Royce in the garage. All and all, a perfect *Best Report* piece.

"First-time writers occasionally complain about our payment rates. I admit we're not in the same league as *Reader's Digest* or *Playboy* when it comes to writers' fees, but we can be a source of good, steady income for someone who really knows our style and the type of stories we want.

"Like most magazines out there, we're not perfect, and once in a while writers have to wait longer than usual to receive payment. But my advice is to hang in there, even if you feel we're treating you unfairly. Remember, the world isn't terribly fair in most aspects of life. The best thing to do is to be understanding. Every writer for *The Best Report* should realize that sooner or later the check will arrive. I'll never forget how one of my best writers did herself in by making a big deal about getting paid several weeks late. She called up furious, yelling, 'I won't be treated this way!' and eventually she wrote a letter of complaint to the Better Business Bureau, carbon-copying our publisher. He, in turn, became furious and told us editors never to use her again. It was really too bad, because she was a good writer; we hardly touched her copy when it came in. And she herself had admitted to us earlier that she needed the work— she had a new baby and lots of expenses.

"So the moral of the story is, Don't burn your bridges, even if you're well within your rights to. You never know when you may need to resume your relationship with a particular magazine."

THE BEST REPORT, 140 East 45th Street, New York, NY 10017; (212) 983-4320.
Frequency of Publication: monthly.
Circulation: 100,000.
Readership: primarily men, average age forty-three.
Available Upon Request: free writer's guidelines and sample copy.
Payment Rate: thirty cents a word.

ANDREA FELD, MANAGING EDITOR, *BRIDE'S*

"Once we assigned a piece for seventy-five dollars and were shocked when the writer submitted a phone bill for three hundred dollars!"

"I'm always surprised when writers call me and ask, 'What is *Bride's* about?' 'What do you publish?' 'Do you ever do financial articles?' Editors don't have the luxury of spending time with writers to acquaint them with their magazine. Most freelancers are working at home—their time is pretty much their own—and many of them forget how busy an editor can get, with meetings, issues in progress, and so on.

"So do your own magazine research. Look at a few issues of *Bride's* on the newsstand or at the library. If you're thinking in terms of 'My Tips on How to Keep a Marriage Happy,' you'll soon see you're on the wrong track—we wouldn't run a piece like that. I'm also surprised by freelancers who submit ideas to me like 'Surviving a Divorce.' Even though the statistics these days indicate that one in every two couples will eventually split up, our readers are about to get married and don't think it'll happen to them. If a writer were to rework her idea into 'How to Divorce-Proof Your Marriage,' she'd have a much better chance.

"You should also know ahead of time which of your expenses are covered by the magazine and which are not; it will save a lot of explaining later on. Once we assigned a piece for seventy-five dollars and were shocked when the writer submitted a phone bill for three hundred dollars! We find that when it comes to research, so much depends on the writer—an experienced person may need to make half as many phone calls as a beginner.

"Another way to make it easier for us to work with you

is to keep a complete fact-checking source list. For instance, we once got a query from a freelancer who'd completed a piece on unusual wedding customs from around the world. It sounded interesting and we would have taken a look at it, except that she hadn't kept her list of sources. Not every magazine is *The New Yorker,* with a large fact-checking staff, and we simply didn't have time to chase down the information. If she'd held onto this list, she might have made a sale to us.

"Above all, don't disappear while you're working on a story for us. Recently I assigned a piece and was counting on getting it in for a particular issue. When the deadline came and went, I called the writer and got her answering machine—*not* a good sign. Eventually she called, very apologetic, saying she was seriously ill and had been hospitalized. Of course, I understood she'd had an emergency, but if you *know* you're seriously sick, or if you're in the midst of a family crisis, have someone tell your editor. The earlier you let her know your situation, the better she'll take it. It'll give her a chance to reassign the story—after all, the magazine can't run blank pages. In the case of the hospitalized freelancer, we'll use her again, but it was so inconvenient to us when she didn't call. Your calendar should be as important to you as a reminder of your magazine deadlines as a lawyer's calendar is to her as a reminder of her court dates.

"Word processors are indispensable for freelance writers, but you have to be five times as careful with a computer as with a typewriter. I've gotten queries addressed to editors of competing magazines! Every editor likes to think your idea was intended for her alone even though, realistically, she knows that's not always going to be the case. Along these lines, *don't* say in your query, 'This idea was just rejected by *Redbook,* but I thought you might want it.' Whenever I see that, I stop reading right there.

"It's smart to get as much input from your editor as you can once you get the assignment. For example, say we ask you to do a piece on hiring a caterer for the wedding. Although you'll be writing a brand-new piece for *Bride's,* you should ask if the assigning editor can send you a photocopy of other stories we've done on the topic—it will help you get an idea of acceptable style and the information previously covered. In addition, along with your own sources, you might ask the editor if she wants you to use an expert she likes, such as the president of the National Caterers Association. She'll also be able to supply you with the names of couples with catering horror stories. Your editor probably has an entire Rolodex of people who are friends of the magazine who'd be willing to give you quotes.

"It is unprofessional for a writer to try to pull the wool over an editor's eyes. Once we assigned a relationship piece to a writer—I was particularly excited about this topic. Then two days before we closed the issue in which the story was scheduled, I spotted a piece by the same writer in another woman's magazine using about half the information and quotes in our story. I was shocked! No editor wants to see her piece ripped off like that.

"Now, I understand that freelancers are in business to make money. They don't have a steady income, and it may be financially important for them to resell their articles or spin off articles using the same research. But writers have to be savvy about *how* they do this and about what information they do and do not use. You should get twice as many quotes and do twice as much research if you think you'll be producing two (or more) articles. In the case of the writer I mentioned, we pulled his article, and on a Friday afternoon I told him, 'I'm counting on you as a professional to do several new interviews for the story by Monday morning,' which he did. He produced a revised piece and we used it—but I don't know that I'd be inclined to work with him again."

BRIDE'S, 350 Madison Avenue, New York, NY 10017; (212) 880-8800.
Frequency of Publication: bimonthly.
Circulation: 450,000.
Readership: brides, median age 23.6; grooms, median age 25.8. Slightly more than one-third of the readers are on their second marriage.
Available Upon Request: free writer's guidelines.
Payment Rate: fifty cents a word.

SUSAN GORDON, SENIOR EDITOR, *CALIFORNIA*

**"[One writer is] forever calling to complain
that she has no money, and she always wants
to be taken out to lunch!"**

"*California* magazine attempts to reflect the lives and concerns of the people of California. There's a complexity to the pieces we do, and there's the hope and expectation that an article in this magazine is one you wouldn't read anywhere else.

"For example, we recently did a story on Jerry Brown and his return to politics. Other magazines have profiled him, certainly, but we feel we have a particular slant that goes beyond the pure objective journalism you might find in, say, *The New York Times Magazine.* There they look for the typical balanced view—you'll read comments from Brown's supporters and detractors and then get his own views. We do that, too, but there's an undercurrent running through the piece, something sly beneath it all. I don't mean we're necessarily going to criticize Jerry Brown, but in the selection of details there'll be a certain *edge.* He's from our own state, after all, and we're looking out for our constituency. We want them to know what they need to know about this man.

"We've occasionally been put in the same category as *Los Angeles Magazine,* but that's much more of a lifestyle magazine—to give you an idea, their July 1989 cover story was 'Pools of the Stars.' *California* covers lifestyle, too, but in a way that really matters to real people. For instance, in 1989 we just won the National Magazine Award for Public Service for our piece on the sleeping pill Halcion. That's what we aspire to. There aren't too many magazines left doing investigative journalism, and that's primarily what we want to be known for.

"We have a lot of terrific writers, and I work with only a couple I find troublesome. There's one freelancer with whom I've worked on four stories. He can write with humor and a nice ironic style, but he can also be precious. He takes himself very seriously, and when it comes to editing his copy, he fights for every word. As a result, I can't assign a piece to him confidently because I know fitting his manuscript into the allocated space will be a battle. Our policy is to work closely with the writer and, as much as possible, let him make the cuts. But this writer always gives reasons why he *can't* make cuts.

"I don't feel I'm arrogant or that I have an I-know-best attitude; I'm respectful of writers. But even the best writers in the best publications occasionally need revision, and it's very hard to work with those people who can't accept that reality.

"I have another writer who drives me up a wall. She's a talented fiction writer who does journalism for us. We often find that people who can make that crossover bring complexity and subtlety to a story—they look for the writerly detail, which gives their pieces a special richness. This writer can do that, and she also suggests good topics. But she requires tremendous personal attention. She's forever calling to complain that she has no money, and she always wants to be taken out to lunch! I was going on my maternity leave in three weeks and she *still* managed to talk me into having lunch with her! There's a real neediness about this writer—she has to feel constantly connected in some way.

"One writer refuses to give up querying us. He writes these long, effusive letters pitching celebrity profiles, even though we don't do celebrity profiles. I tell him this again and again, but it doesn't stop him from sending these endless proposals. We finally did publish him—in a satirical way—in our front-of-the-book 'New West' section of short humor and news pieces. We put one of his queries in a box—the item went on and on about how 'my story will take *California* readers right into the heart of Hollywood. . . .' It was comical; it looked like it had been written as a parody. But believe it or not, a few months later he wrote us a similar letter, which we *also* published.

"One freelancer I *love* working with is someone I've never met in person. When I assigned him his first piece—a travel story he'd proposed—I had never even read his stuff, but he came highly recommended and had good credentials. And when I received his manuscript, it may have been the first time in my twelve years as an editor that I felt, This is perfect. It did everything I hoped a piece would do. It dealt with his experiences at a mountain-climbing school in the Sierra Nevadas, and he told a complicated story in a sustained narrative with lots of wonderful detail. He brought in his own feelings, and they drew you into the story: you got a real sense of what the place felt like, looked like, and smelled like, as well as a clear picture of the other characters from the trip. It was a powerful and impressive piece.

"Of course, after reading it many times, I had a few small suggestions for the writer on how to tighten it. We worked on it carefully together, and it was a good experience for both of us. He seemed comfortable in accepting— and rejecting—my suggestions, and there was a terrific resolution. It remains my favorite travel piece of all the ones we've run in *California,* and I've just given the writer another big assignment.

"The main thing with him, of course, is that he's a fantastically talented writer! But also important is the fact that he seems like a truly decent person, someone who's well-balanced."

CALIFORNIA, 11601 Wilshire Boulevard, Los Angeles, CA 90025; (213) 479-6511.
Frequency of Publication: monthly.
Circulation: 350,000.
Readership: Men and women, ages thirty-two to fifty.
Payment Rate: fifty cents a word, more for established writers.

KATE WHITE, EDITOR-IN-CHIEF, *CHILD*

**"No matter . . . how much candy you drop
off at [an editor's] office on Valentine's Day,
your charm will take you just so far."**

"Because I've stayed very active as a freelance writer throughout my career as a magazine editor—I've also worked at *Mademoiselle, Glamour,* and *Family Weekly*— I've seen both sides. Most editors tend to stop writing once they reach the articles-editor level, but I've continued— and being a writer helps me see what drives editors crazy.

"What influences my relationship with a writer the most? It all comes down to good writing. No matter how wonderful you are to an editor, or how much candy you drop off at her office on Valentine's Day, your charm will take you just so far. After that, it boils down to your work.

"That's not to say that there aren't things you can do as a freelancer to make your working relationship with an editor easier. For example, editors can make mistakes when it comes to assignments, and it helps if you can get around their foibles. At *Mademoiselle*, editors would routinely give incredibly long lead times to writers. Because we went after wonderful writers like Mary Gordon and Jay McInerney, we were willing to wait two or three months for their pieces to come in. But that system created problems. Editors were also casual about giving—or, rather, *not* giving—letters of assignment. A writer might come in to discuss a story and would take notes, but he wouldn't get a formal assignment letter. So then a couple of months later he'd start to work on the article, whip out his legal pad containing his notes from the meeting, and see buzzwords like *energy* and *communication*—and not really know what the editor wanted.

"Here at *Child* I find that shortening writers' deadlines to about six weeks and giving them assignment letters result in better pieces. If you as a freelancer are working with an editor who doesn't give you such a letter, ask for one, or write your own, send it in, and have the editor confirm what's in it. Know what the working title of the article is—I never give an assignment to a writer without one because it helps give him structure. If your editor hasn't told you the story's working title, call her and ask. And be sure to request a brief meeting with the editor sometime before the story is due, so you can update her and discuss any problems or changes.

"I appreciate it when freelancers really think things through and help us shape the story. One of our writers, for instance, was assigned a piece we called 'Will Your

Child Be Happily Married?' She sent us back the most beautiful, fantastic letter outlining three possible ways to go with the story. She showed us it was too broad a topic and helped us narrow it down—and eventually submitted a great piece.

"It's good if you can work with an editor who's high up on the masthead. If you work with an associate editor, there are so many layers between you and the top person that your immediate editor won't have the clout to rescue you if there's a problem with your piece. That's why it's smart to submit your first query to a senior editor or the articles editor—the most senior person who would logically receive such submissions.

"But if you *do* find yourself in a bad situation with your immediate editor, *don't* try to circumvent her by appealing to her superior. When I was at *Mademoiselle,* I didn't line-edit; I delegated everything. Whenever there was a problem and the writer contacted me directly to straighten it out, I didn't like it. This sort of behavior on the part of the writer annoys everyone.

"At *Child* we have a very small staff, and along with being the editor-in-chief, I also assign pieces. I have only so much time to do everything, and what really bothers me is when a writer calls me when I'm not available and leaves no message. It's a monumental burden to return everyone's call, and sometimes the writer is calling simply to say her story will be a day late or that she needs tearsheets of her article. So if you're calling, leave a message as to what it's about. You'll often get faster service that way than if you wait for me or one of my assistants to return your call.

"When you're trying to write for *Child,* remember that you're dealing with a *national* readership. Some writers make their ideas or their stories so parochial. For instance, I gave a woman an assignment that necessitated quotes from a baby expert; instead, she interviewed her own pedi-

atrician. My reaction was, Have you *never* read a magazine? Most experts have done research in their field or are affiliated with a university. That seemed very basic to me, yet this writer didn't contact the right person.

"In another case, I was told about a young mother in Pennsylvania who wanted to write for me. My expectations were not high, but I sighed and said, 'Okay, I'll talk to her.' Frankly, her ideas weren't great, but she was extremely professional—she really knew the protocol of working with an editor. I gave her an assignment, and she not only interviewed great people from all over the country but also followed the letter of the law regarding what I asked her to do. She is one of my few successful out-of-town freelancers without a newspaper background.

"I suggest that potential *Child* writers go through magazine articles with a highlighter. Use them as models for what you want to do. Too often freelancers kid themselves about the amount of work required for a publishable piece. Look at the heft of the research found in a typical article; look at the number of people interviewed. It all takes more time and effort than you think.

"People who don't know us lump us with *Parents* and *Parenting,* but our readers are more upscale and more educated, with a median income of $46,000. We're the 'Thirtysomething' audience. We do service stories, of course, but we're mainly concerned with exploring the complexity of parenting today. I'm looking for stories that go beyond the basics, something with an edge, a 'hook.' For instance, instead of running the usual babysitting piece—'24 Things to Ask a Babysitter Before You Hire Her'—we ran a compilation of thirty parents' horror stories under the title 'Babysitters from Hell.' Instead of something on fostering creativity, we did 'How Not to Kill Your Child's Creativity.' Create a catchy title or flip a tried-and-true idea on its ear. Very rarely do writers come to us with that, so when someone does, it's great."

CHILD, 110 Fifth Avenue, New York, NY 10011; (212) 463-1000.
Frequency of Publication: ten times a year.
Circulation: 350,000.
Readership: parents of children up to twelve years old, but mostly under five.
Payment Rate: one thousand dollars minimum.

JUDITH COYNE, SENIOR EDITOR, *GLAMOUR*

"Demonstrate to [your editor] that you won't have a cardiac infarction at the sight of a pencil mark on your manuscript."

"Today, fifty-one years after its debut on the newsstand, *Glamour* is becoming more sophisticated as its readers have become more sophisticated. The *Glamour* reader is someone who grew up during a time of great opportunity for women. Our aim is to help her celebrate where she's come from and the life she can expect to live. For example, we're beyond the question, Can you combine a career and a family? The reader knows she can. What she gets from us is information on how to do it better.

"To give you an idea: we run a lot of pieces dealing with relationships and sex. Two of the most popular articles we've done recently are 'The Marriage Revolution: What Men Want Now'—which explores how men in their twenties differ from their fathers in what they expect—and a piece called 'Can You Be Too Good in Bed?' I think the premise of the piece really corresponded to readers' lives:

given that the average woman has had a fair number of relationships, how will her newest lover deal with her sexual experience? This is a good example of a *Glamour* piece in that it takes a pro-woman stance: your life is your own and you have nothing to apologize for sexually. What the article explores is the question of where you go from there.

"We also like to take chances with pieces, choosing subjects and formats that may surprise writers who've never taken a careful look at *Glamour*. A perfect example from a couple of years ago was 'Slashed!,' by Susan Edmiston, a contributing editor. It was the story of Marla Hansen, the woman who came from a small Texas town to become a model in New York, only to have her face slashed by her ex-landlord's henchmen. The story had a lot of dramatic elements: a beautiful young woman living a glamorous life, the horrible experience she endures, and finally her triumph over it. It was a terrific piece; I wish we had narrative as strong as that to publish tomorrow, and the next day, and the next.

"Another aspect of *Glamour* is our emphasis on reporting pieces. We've won a number of national awards, most recently for a piece we ran in late 1988 called 'Hiding Hilary: A True Story of Love, Divorce, and Sexual Abuse,' by Bob Trebilcock. It was the story of Elizabeth Morgan, the Washington plastic surgeon who was convinced that her ex-husband was sexually abusing their daughter. After getting nowhere in litigation, she eventually put the child into hiding, only to be put in jail herself for contempt of court. When we did our article, she'd been in jail about eighteen months. A lot of other magazines picked up on the story after that and she became a *cause célèbre,* but we were the first. I like that and aspire to it.

"The stories I've mentioned were all executed by first-class writers. Besides being excellent reporters and stylists, they're also professionals who are a pleasure to deal with. That's important, I think. Magazines generate a lot of their own ideas, and although we're always looking for *new* writers, it's also true that I often bring an idea to someone who's not only talented but has proved to be dependable and good to work with.

"I appreciate writers who know how to keep conversations focused and to-the-point while minimizing the hassles that, as an editor, you may impose on them. Of course, difficult discussions *are* sometimes necessary—maybe I've made a big cut or line change that, in the author's opinion, hurts rather than helps the piece. Maybe the author thinks I've asked for material that's unnecessary. Maybe the author thinks I'm an idiot. Regardless, I believe it's smart for you, the writer, to start out by saying what you *liked* about the editing. Obviously, the editor feels that what she did *improved* the piece, so acknowledge that. One writer I've worked with usually opens the discussion of the editing by saying some variation of, 'Looks good. I like it. It's tight. It's smooth.' She may be just cozying me along till she gets to the part she hated—but that's okay. She's acknowledging that she knows the editor has a function, and she's showing she respected my effort. (It goes without saying, of course, that the editor should show the same respect for the writer.) The short version of this speech is treat the editor the way you'd like to be treated. Demonstrate to her that you won't have a cardiac infarction at the sight of a pencil mark on your manuscript, and chances are you'll end up agreeing on the major points you want to raise.

"One thing I hate to see in a writer is a hard sell. Basically, I don't like saying no to people, but once I've said an idea isn't right for us and explained why, I wish the writer would take me at my word and move on to something else (or just say good-bye or that she'll talk to me about something else soon). A writer who keeps pushing me *may* eventually get me to grumble, 'Okay, send me a query on it,' but that just leads to unnecessary work for the writer; it rarely changes the decision. And the whole encounter leaves me with a knot in my stomach.

"One thing that really impresses me in a writer is when I ask for certain specific revisions, and the writer not only deals with those but also shows she's thought the piece through by initiating other changes herself. She's made the effort to present the best second draft possible, not just gotten the editor's objections out of the way.

"I'm turned off by writers who accept an invitation to lunch (or, occasionally, ask me to lunch) but don't bring ideas to the table. If the editor is courting you, that's one thing (though it's still preferable if you've got *something* to contribute). But if it's just a regular business lunch, coming up empty is bad form. Some writers take the attitude, Well, the magazine knows what it wants; dreaming up near misses is just a waste of my time. I disagree. The editor may not be able to use what you present but may be sparked to think of something else that *would* work. Or she may add a different spin, or a new piece of research, to what you thought of. Even if none of the above happens, she gets to see how your mind works and gets a better sense of your natural interests, which helps *your* name float to the top of her brain when she's assigning something. In any case, give the editor a break. Lunch is a major commitment of her time and attention; she should have something to show for it besides the bill."

GLAMOUR, 350 Madison Avenue, New York, NY 10017; (212) 880-8800
Frequency of Publication: monthly.
Circulation: 2.3 million.
Readership: women, average age twenty-six; 50 percent are single, 50 percent married.
Available Upon Request: free writer's guidelines.
Payment Rate: one dollar a word minimum.

DIANNE PARTIE LANGE, EDITOR-IN-CHIEF, *HEALTH*

**"There's a fine line between pestering an
editor just enough and becoming a pest."**

"Because we're a small staff, I wear several hats. Besides
being editor-in-chief, I also act as senior beauty editor and
senior medical editor, the latter because I'm a former nurse
and have a particular interest in medicine. I read medical
journals for fun! That's why I can often track stories before
they break in the regular press.

"Sometimes I'll jump in and assign a story to save time.
Then, when it comes in, I may pass it on to another editor
to edit—which writers hate! I know what it's like to be on
that side—I was a freelancer myself for eight years. If a
writer calls me a lot about a story, I *understand* her anxiety.
As much as I want to give writers a quick response, I can't
always, but I *know* someone is waiting, thinking it's one
more day of my hating her piece. I realize writers need to
get paid, that the gas and electric bills won't wait. It's hard
being a freelancer. I used to work seven days a week doing
that—but I do that as editor-in-chief too!

"I once heard an editor of another magazine say at a
luncheon that at her publication they assign a lot of stories
to anyone and everyone. When I was an editor at *Self*, it
was just the opposite: We were *so* cautious in assigning
pieces. Every writer—even veteran writers—had to be
okayed by the editor-in-chief. I don't do that here at
Health. I trust my editors will make wise decisions about
assigning stories—after all, *they* are the ones who'll have to
struggle to make the piece work. And now, after having
worked with me for a year, they know I'll be hard on them
if the piece *doesn't*.

"I think writers believe editors are very cavalier about
killing stories. The truth is we *hate* to kill pieces. We put

time, energy, and research into every story, and sometimes it's even been scheduled for a particular issue. If the piece comes from a writer with whom you have a relationship, it's especially hard to tell him without hurting his ego that the writing didn't make it or that there was inadequate research.

"It doesn't pay to make enemies in this business—I may want to use this writer for another kind of piece. I talk with my editors if they're stuck or having problems with a writer and try to help them resolve the situation. A writer who does a lousy piece for me today may make great progress five years from now and become someone whose work I'd love to see in the magazine.

"In the time I've been at *Health* I can think of only three writers who got upset about the way their story was handled. We try to be very gentle with freelancers. For example, when I took over, there was a piece I inherited that had been assigned by a former editor. By my definition the piece was terrible, and because the writer had made a few sales under the old regime, he didn't understand why I killed it. Due to the particular circumstances, I didn't feel it was fair to pay him our standard 20 percent kill fee, so I gave him 50 percent. We talked a lot about the piece and what I felt was wrong with it, and I promised I'd try him again. I did, and he's turned out to be one of our best writers.

"We had one true horror story involving a writer. He submitted to one of our editors an unfixable piece—we killed it for good reason. We had even provided him with some of the research. He became *very* angry at the editor, even though she had spent *hours* on the phone with him, walking him through the piece. After all *that,* he took the piece, including the research *we* had provided, and sold it to one of our competitors! Needless to say, I'll never work with that writer again. And don't forget, editors talk and names go around—'Oh, *that* guy!' and 'I used her a couple of years ago—never again!' I treat writers with graciousness and respect, even when it's hard. Writers should do the same with their editors.

"There are other little quirky things freelancers do that bother me, like call me all the time. I can't find time to talk to even my best friends! It's true that the squeaky wheel *will* eventually wear you down, but there's a fine line between pestering an editor just enough and becoming a pest.

"I also dislike when writers underestimate the sophistication of our magazine. There's a lot of research and solid information in *Health,* and yet many writers have the attitude, 'Oh, your audience doesn't want to know about that' or 'That's too technical for women.' The research we get in is often too 'soft,' too superficial. A lot of writers think that every psychology story is 'Five Ways to Get Out of a Bad Mood.' But nothing could be further from the truth. In our March 1989 issue our lead story was on pollution. We sent a writer to Arizona, where she worked with 'garbologists' and went through the dumps to try to come up with what our garbage reveals about our behavior as well as about toxic waste. A companion piece, on what's in the air and how it affects us, was written by one of our best freelancers, Peter Jaret.

"What makes him so good? He's extraordinarily reliable when it comes to meeting deadlines, as well as a solid researcher—he's not afraid to call a lot of people to find the right source of information. He's so good that he even tips us off when a story we've given him isn't going as we expected.

"For instance, I assigned him a story on the popularity of taking vitamin E as an antioxidant, to counter the effects of pollution in the body. I wanted him to go into a lot of health-food stores—he's based in California—to see if there was any validity to using vitamin E this way. At first he thought it was a great idea, but then he did his legwork and found there was no story there. He came back with a brand-new focus for the piece and I said, 'Great, go ahead.' I trust him completely, and he's earned that trust. He's just a delight to work with. He only calls when he needs to, and if he has to do a revise (and even someone of his caliber does occasionally), he's very willing. Above all, he has integrity. The best writers do."

HEALTH, 3 Park Avenue, New York, NY 10016; (212) 779-6200.
Frequency of Publication: ten times a year.
Circulation: 1.1 million.
Readership: women; average age thirty-nine.
Available Upon Request: free writer's and research guidelines.
Payment Rate: one dollar a word.

NELSON ALDRICH, JR., ARTICLES EDITOR, *LEAR'S*

"We've had manuscripts come in that . . .
are messy in a way that a third-grader
wouldn't hand in to Miss O'Leary."

"I left the magazine business as an editor in 1976 to free-lance—I still write for *New England Monthly, The New York Review of Books,* and others. Since returning to editing—I joined *Lear's* in October 1988—I've been astonished and shocked at the quality of manuscripts that come in these days. It's as though writers—including good, well-known writers—refuse to take any responsibility for what they write! We've had manuscripts come in that might as well be notes. They're messy in a way that a third-grader wouldn't hand in to Miss O'Leary. It's incredible! And it's not just at this magazine. I've taken an informal poll among my friends at other magazines, and they say the same thing.

"There are reasons for it, I suppose. One colleague at *Lear's* believes that because there's more money in book writing these days, professional writers tend to treat magazines as secondary sources of income, something that doesn't deserve fully worked, fully written manuscripts. If a magazine pays, let's say, two thousand dollars for two thousand words, it makes a lot of difference to a writer if he spends two months or two weeks writing that article. And if he knows it takes four weeks to do a fully responsible job, why not try to get away with doing it in two? There's always a chance the editors will look at it and say, 'It's okay; we can work on it.' I really wonder whether that's the not-so-subliminal reasoning in the freelancer's mind.

"Is the stuff we get junk? No. If it were simply junk, you could throw it out and say to yourself, I made a mistake; I won't ask this writer again. Instead an article might be filled with dazzling insights and vivid writing, but it's a *mess,* an intolerable rat's nest of sloppy syntax, typos, and broken-back structure—everything Miss O'Toole found objectionable in your freshman comp courses at Podunk U.! A manuscript comes in that looks and reads like the beginning of a game of Pickup Sticks! The sticks themselves may be pretty, but you've got to *make* something happen with them. I swear to God this wasn't the case ten or twelve years ago. Writers had more pride in their work then.

"It's almost as though writers expect *you,* the editor, to do their work for them. It might be that they've had experiences with heavy-handed magazine editors and their thinking is, They'll rewrite me anyway, so why not just turn it in as is.

"The attitude is defiant, calculated, grudging, a *je m'en foutisme*—fuck-you-ism. And I'm exercised about it because, as a freelance writer myself, I've always tried to do the best I could. If I write something, it's because I want what I say to be published. I want to exercise maximum control over my words, my syntax, my structure—and my editor! I want to please him; I want him to be happy when he opens the envelope. I don't want to hand in a piece of shit. When I write, I want my meaning to get out there. I'm surprised—and appalled—that people are so careless of their meanings, that they would surrender the expression of those meanings to someone else, that is, their editor. That's where economics comes in—'I can't make money doing it properly, so the hell with it. I'll do it any way I can.'

"There's a freelance writer whom I personally like, and we commissioned him to write a story he asked to do about his mother. I've never *seen* such a mess! Reading it was like a drive in a four-wheel vehicle going down the Grand Canyon. Here it wasn't so much a case of carelessness as that he had no business writing about his mother in the first place—he was so conflicted in his feelings about her that he was having a nervous breakdown over her on the *page*! Frances [Lear, editor-in-chief] really wanted to try to run the piece, and another *Lear's* editor had to work very hard to make it publishable. But the writer was outraged when he saw what was done with it. As far as he was concerned, we had *raped* his mother! It was a terrible scene. Still, this was unusual. Most people who don't take editing well are inexperienced.

"There are many writers who approach the magazine with some misconceptions about what it is. The biggest is that *Lear's* is a typical 'women's magazine,' that is, a kind of sentimental complaint box for all the victims of the female gender. Apparently, as early as the late seventeenth century there was a certain genre of literature called the 'injured-woman narrative.' Even back then it was a best-seller, and it evolved into such things as the books by the Brontës. There is still all over the Western world a kind of morbid self-consciousness among women, which ranges from an obsessive concern with appearance to a savage hatred of their inadequacies. A certain relief from this condition seems to come from dwelling on the injuries suffered at the hands of men, society, children, mothers—and this is provided in many women's magazines.

"However, *our* reader is a grown-up human being who has put behind her the shattering self-consciousness of adolescence. She has found herself to be—possibly after some suffering of one sort or another—a person of power, resourcefulness, imagination, and humor. She wants to make a difference in the world, especially for what she thinks of as 'posterity.' Freelancers should understand this, and I'd like to see them take this magazine even more seriously as a vehicle for good reporting on political, social, economic, and cultural conflicts. Almost any manuscript a writer would send to *Esquire* or *Rolling Stone* or *The New York Times Magazine* should be considered for *Lear's*."

LEAR'S, 655 Madison Avenue, New York, NY 10021; (212) 888-0007.
Frequency of Publication: monthly.
Circulation: 350,000
Readership: female; median age forty-five.
Payment Rate: one dollar a word minimum.

ANNE SUMMERS, EDITOR-AT-LARGE, *MS.*

"People have to understand the balance between working with an editor and driving her insane."

"I don't work directly with writers that much anymore, but I did when I first came to the magazine—in fact, I assigned the entire February 1988 issue. I was in the process of changing the direction of *Ms.*, and it needed my direct touch. Now the staff knows what I want, although I've assigned a few pieces in recent issues. When it's a cover story or a subject I have a particular interest in, the assigning editor and I get the writer into the office to discuss it. I find that helps avoid misunderstanding, and it assures us that we and the writer are on the same wavelength.

"For example, I personally assigned a piece in our September 1989 issue, an essay on women in Ireland. It's very political, and it coincides with the twentieth anniversary of the British occupation of Northern Ireland. I also had a big hand in a major medical story we ran, called 'The Miracle Baby,' about an infant born at twenty-three weeks. It was important not only from a medical standpoint but also as it related to *Roe* v. *Wade* (which, until the July 1989 Supreme Court decision in the *Webster* case, legally allowed abortion up until the twenty-fourth week after conception).

"The magazine has changed in two major ways. First, we have an expanded editorial agenda, with a larger number of topics to be covered than ever before, including regular features on technology, style (in a column called 'Clobber,' which is British slang for apparel), and gardening and the environment ('Earthly Delights'). We're also doing more political stories—*Ms.* couldn't cover politics in the days it was owned by a foundation.

"The tone of the magazine has changed as well. I feel that *Ms.* must be accessible to *any* woman, even if she doesn't call herself a feminist. If someone thinks the status of women is an important issue, she ought to be reading *Ms.* We've gotten harder about the subject of politics—it's time to stop pussyfooting around!—but at the same time the magazine's 'voice' has gotten softer. In fact, we seek a *diversity* of voices, but within the framework I've just described.

"What I'm looking for are really good 'reads,' more narrative journalism. For example, we have a piece coming up that investigates the growth of environmental toxins and their impact on children's health. Along with solid reporting, the article has a strong narrative flavor.

"*Ms.* is a genre of its own—there are no real models for what we do. *Esquire* does it a bit; so does *Harper's*. Our stories cover a wide range of issues, and they have something of an edge to them. We're reporting on the world as it is while, at the same time, advocating for change. We're also a *reader's* magazine; there's a lot of good reading in *Ms.*

"We've been getting an incredible number of queries and manuscripts on personal subjects—relationships with mothers, letting go of children as they grow up, the death of a parent. There might be some good ideas there, and I'm sure writing about these subjects is very cathartic, but we can only publish one death-of-a-parent story a year. However, I *do* want good submissions for our new 'Intimacies' column, featuring first-person relationship stories. But these relationships must be discussed broadly, as they relate to other areas of the writer's life.

"If there's a turnoff for me where it comes to freelance writers, it's when they put inaccurate or incomplete information in their stories and depend too heavily on our fact-checking department. Actually, I wasn't comfortable at first with the need for fact checking—I come from a newspaper tradition where it is simply assumed the writer has checked her own facts. I'm still shocked by the number of TKs [to come] I find in the average submission. I feel that we pay writers good money and that our research department shouldn't be responsible for doing the writers' work. But I've softened on this issue, and for writers who contribute frequently to *Ms.*, we do use our research department to help them.

"Another turnoff: writers who won't allow their copy to be edited! The less experienced the writers, the worse they are about it, and I understand their feelings—as a beginning writer I thought every one of my commas was sacred! But we at *Ms.* care a great deal about the quality of our work, and we won't make changes without the writer's consent. We will show her a computer printout of her story, although we don't show the cuts or additions to make the story fit on the page—there's simply no time for that. We've had writers complain about the sudden appearance of a cliché in their story, but sometimes we need to add things at 11:00 P.M.

"There are also writers who drive us crazy by calling us all the time. People have to understand the balance between working with an editor and driving her insane. Some writers bug us about really trivial things. I just won't use certain people again; life's too short.

"Then there are the good writers. They follow the assignment and turn in their stories on time, and their stories don't require a huge editorial input. What they submit to us is just a good piece of writing. In my experience as a journalist I've learned that you give the editor what she wants, you do it well, and the story gets published essentially untouched.

"Still, a writer may have given an editor everything she's asked for and the manuscript isn't right. Therefore, freelancers should be prepared to work with the editor. Just because you've written the piece doesn't mean it's the end of the job."

MS., 1 Times Square, New York, NY 10036; (212) 719-9800.
Frequency of Publication: bimonthly.
Circulation: 550,000.
Readership: women; median age thirty-three.

Available Upon Request: free writer's guidelines.
Payment Rate: "according to a writer's experience and expertise."

ELLEN SWEET, MANAGING EDITOR, *NEW CHOICES FOR THE BEST YEARS*

"When I first joined the magazine, a friend of mine . . . said, 'Send me the magazine— but in a plain, brown wrapper!'"

"A lot of confusion arises with writers these days because they're not aware of the changes at the magazine. We went from *50 Plus* to *New Choices for the Best Years* in January 1989, after having been bought by *Reader's Digest*. *Reader's Digest* thoroughly researches *everything* before making any changes, and they found that half the readers liked the original name of the magazine and half didn't, so they looked for a new title that wouldn't alienate so many people. I understood that thinking: When I first joined the magazine, a friend of mine in her forties said, 'Send me the magazine—but in a plain, brown wrapper!'

"In the days when we were *50 Plus,* we were basically a news and advocacy magazine. Now we're more of a lifestyle and service magazine, focusing on healthy, busy people with more time and disposable income to lead an active life. We're aimed at the forty-five-to-sixty-four age group, and our subjects range from travel to health, from sex to sports, from relationships to profiles of 'real people.' Yet there are still many writers who assume our readership is sixty-five and older, and they often suggest stories about 'remarkable' older people. But the reality of who our reader is is a far cry from the stereotypical image of the decrepit old person in a nursing home.

"Health is a major focus of the magazine, and I really dislike it when a writer doesn't do sufficient research, particularly in this area. I get annoyed when freelancers use secondary sources—such as magazines only slightly more specialized than ours—to get their information.

"For instance, I made an assignment to a writer and provided her with some research information, citing studies that had been done at two universities. She used that information, but when we fact-checked it, we found out it was wrong. I had assumed the writer would go directly to the source and review the actual studies, but she didn't—and our fact checker had to devote a lot of time to getting the right data. The writer may have felt a sense of closure when she turned in her piece, but it was just the beginning as far as we were concerned. She took a shortcut that ultimately created a lot of extra work for us.

"Besides health pieces, I occasionally edit travel stories at the magazine, and some writers will call and say, 'I'm going to Spain this summer. Do you want any articles about it?' I hate that approach—it only makes me jealous that *I'm* not going! The ideal way to propose a story to me, whether it's travel or any other category, is to *send* one or two queries, with backup clips relating to the ideas you're proposing. And think about what *our* reason would be for doing this article. Your query must be able to answer that question, as well as why *you* should be the one to write the piece.

"I really wonder about freelance writers who take everything their editor says at face value, even when it's illogical to do so. I have one freelancer who's a nutritionist—basically she's an academic writer. She suggested doing a piece on osteoporosis, and I sent her an assignment letter which, I admit, I had been too rushed to proofread. The letter asked for a piece of *twenty thousand* words instead of *two thousand*—and she delivered twenty thousand words! So, read your assignment letter carefully, and call if there are any questions. Of course, this is an extreme example, but it's still a good idea to talk to your editor if you're not sure about how to proceed. This will avoid the I-thought-you-wanted-me-to-emphasize-X-and-not-Y discussion after you submit your piece.

"By the same token, if you hit a snag while doing your story, I want to know about it, especially if it will change the focus or tone. For example, I may assign you an upbeat story on women returning to work after fifty, and if you discover in the course of your research that it's *not* an upbeat story, you'd better let me know right away. It may not simply be an assumption on my part that the picture is a rosy one but actually a *mandate* of the magazine to show something positive.

"Even the most innocent-sounding stories can cause problems. Recently I asked a freelancer to do a story on adult children returning to the nest, and we both thought initially that there'd be plenty of examples of families willing to be interviewed and photographed. As it turned out, five out of six of the families the writer found refused to have their picture taken and would only agree to be quoted off the record. Although these five families wouldn't talk about themselves, they *did* agree to offer coping tips for others in their situation. After discussing the story with me, I had the writer go ahead with that angle, and we used illustrations instead of photos to accompany the piece. It worked out fine, but it was important that I knew about these changes as early as I did.

"Often a writer for *New Choices* will sit back and wait for the editor to call her—and she doesn't understand why it doesn't happen. You may think your editor has written you off and she hasn't, but she *might* have some serious reservations about you without your knowing it. It's good to get an honest evaluation from your editor. I believe there should be a postmortem after your article has been published, especially if there were problems along the way. You might say to the editor, 'I realize the piece didn't go so well. How could we have made it easier?' Get her to be frank with you—the best editors are very direct. There may simply have been some miscommunication on your last story. It's a competitive world, and a writer can't afford to go down dead ends with editors."

NEW CHOICES FOR THE BEST YEARS, 28 West 23rd Street, New York, NY 10010; (212) 633-4600.
Frequency of Publication: monthly.
Circulation: 600,000
Readership: 68 percent female, 32 percent male; from forty-five to sixty-four years old.
Available Upon Request: free writer's guidelines with an SASE.
Payment Rate: approximately one dollar a word.

LARRY SMITH, MANAGING EDITOR, *PARADE*

"[Freelance writing] is a brutal, thankless life!"

"If anything bothers me about writers, it's getting a proposal from someone who hasn't read and familiarized himself with the magazine. It's purely foolish to call me or write in to pitch some idea that's too tightly focused for an audience of our depth and breadth—*Parade*'s circulation is more than 33 million, and our readership is twice that. I tell writers to think of an idea that might be appropriate for a segment of *60 Minutes* and go beyond that; our audience is much larger than theirs. We say, 'Think big, but think *focused.'*

"We're looking for *universal* themes. A proposal for a story about the hundredth anniversary of the Johnstown Flood or about a small New York City dance company just isn't going to make it in *Parade.* On the other hand, it *is* possible to take a tightly pinpointed story and make it work for us. For instance, one of our writers did a piece a few years ago on Weirton, West Virginia, where a steel mill was on the verge of closing down and the townspeople were trying to buy it. Eventually they did and made a success of it. That was an example of a single place, yet the story had to do with people's livelihoods, with *survival,* and those are themes everyone is interested in.

"Another thing that concerns me is when a writer sends in a two-page proposal. Any time someone needs more than three paragraphs to pitch an idea it means she hasn't thought the idea through. Sometimes a proposal comes to us in the shape of an outline, but basically we find that the tighter the proposal, the better. Any plot, any thought, begins with a single sentence. If in your own mind you can boil down your idea to one sentence, that's good.

"I like writers who can work independently—we don't want to hold their hands, although some writers expect us to. One woman who got an assignment from us, for example, called our executive editor after she'd done a taped interview with the subject of her story—she wanted to play the editor the tape! He said, 'Write it up! That's what you're getting paid to do!' The piece she turned in, I might add, was a disaster. It'll be the last time we work with her.

"Never, when handing in your manuscript, say or write on a cover letter, 'I really like this piece' or 'This story is one of the best I've ever done.' It tells us the piece is probably weak and that the writer is feeling insecure about it— that's my two-cent psychology lesson.

"Generally speaking, the key to success as a freelancer is good contacts—and I realize it's hard to make them over the transom. How does a new writer do it? One way is to get an introduction to an editor through another published writer. A second way is to try to find out who at the magazine is the best person to contact—it's not always evident from the masthead—and make an effort to develop a relationship with that person.

"But contacts or no, the most important thing is to have good ideas—they're the lodestone of any magazine. At the same time, coming up with a steady stream of good ideas is about the hardest thing to do. I'd suggest that a smart, aspiring freelancer go back to popular magazines from the forties, fifties, and sixties, and review the ideas there. For heaven's sake, don't plagiarize, but try to get *inspiration* from them! There's nothing new under the sun—everything is constantly being reworked in some way, and magazine articles can be dressed up differently or vary with the times. I think the best way to get ideas is by looking at ideas that have already been sold to somebody. But you need to look beyond the obvious and give the idea a new twist. *Parade* gets six proposals on acid rain a month; try something fresh.

"At *Parade* we like to think you're a professional—we deal with people on professional terms. Everyone has a shot. We work with new writers right out of the gate all the way to pros like Norman Mailer and Carl Sagan. When an idea we like comes in, an assignment is made, a contract is sent out, and the writer is expected to deliver the manuscript in the requisite time. Very often we ask for two to three rewrites, but the writer is always involved, right through to the page proofs.

"A staple of *Parade* is our celebrity interviews—over the years we've done a lot of them and still do. But we don't just write about a celebrity; we try to go deeper and find out what really matters to the person, what makes him or her unique. We try to get subjects to reveal themselves in a way they don't in a typical interview. For instance, we recently ran a profile of Lena Horne in which she had some startling revelations about what it's like to be seventy-one and wishing for a man. To come up with a really great profile, the interviewer has to be extremely skilled and truly care about the subject. Two masters of the genre are Dotson Rader and Tom Seligson, both of whom write regularly for *Parade*.

"The way we assess a submission for the magazine is whether we, the editors, like it—we don't distinguish between our audience and ourselves. *Parade* doesn't talk down to its readers in any way.

"None of my comments about writing for *Parade*, by the way, are said in a scornful manner. I think there's only one thing harder in the world than being a freelance writer and that's being a freelance photographer. My sympathy and warmest wishes go out to all writers. They constantly have to scratch and scramble to get ideas and then sell them to editors. Their payments never keep up with the times. It's a brutal, thankless life! If you can make a living at it, great— I tried it myself for a time and didn't even come close."

PARADE, 750 Third Avenue, New York, NY 10017; (212) 573-7000.
Frequency of Publication: weekly.
Circulation: 33.3 million; Sunday magazine appears in 320 U.S. newspapers.
Readership: 49 percent men; 51 percent women; median age forty.
Available Upon Request: free writer's guidelines.
Payment Rate: one dollar a word minimum.

ANN PLESHETTE MURPHY, EDITOR-IN-CHIEF, *PARENTS*

"The ones who can't write their way out of a paper bag also tend to be the ones who call you forty times a week."

"There's more to a magazine than just the stories it publishes. There's also an *attitude,* a *culture* that many writers don't take the time to discern. *Parents* is no exception. We take a generous view of parents and children—we're respectful of both. If you read the magazine, you'll see what I'm talking about.

"I don't want articles that make fun of children, and I do get a few where the stories just cross the line, where the humor is at the expense of the child. For example, I recently received on spec a humor piece, dealing with how the writer's son developed a fear of going to bed. It all started after she'd been reading him fairy tales filled with ghosts and demons. Well, my feeling was, why was she reading frightening fairy tales to a three-year-old in the first place? The story didn't make it.

"While we're not the Pollyanna of child-development news—in fact, we deal with tough subjects—we have a friendly, helpful attitude toward the reader. If, say, your style of writing is very sophisticated or your specialty is semicynical writing, I would say *Parents* is not for you. The magazine combines the feeling of confiding in a friend and talking with an expert. We're looking for stories with the *common touch.* If something is too 'yuppified,' it might not work for us.

"What makes *Parents* unusual is that we're a mass-market, single-topic magazine. Our readers have an obsession—their families and children—yet they also want advice about other aspects of their lives: fashion, beauty, food, personal finance.

"Do you have to be a parent to write for *Parents*? Not necessarily, but most of our writers are. It seems that until you have kids of your own, there are lots of other things you'd rather write about, and then once you have kids, that's *all* you want to write about. The I've-been-there approach appeals to our readers—they respond to someone who understands them.

"Of course it doesn't necessarily work the other way: just because you *are* a parent doesn't mean you're a good writer! For instance, we have a regular feature called 'It Worked for Me!,' in which someone describes a problem and how he or she solved it. The people who've written for the column run the gamut from our top contributors to unknowns whose stuff comes over the transom. We're looking for real voices, so when the writer is mediocre but has a terrific story to tell, we'll often buy the piece knowing it will require more work; so far it hasn't been a struggle for us.

"I can also offer encouragement by saying that we're not overly concerned with getting big-name writers into the magazine—it's really more important to us that your voice somehow touch the reader. For example, a complete amateur approached us not long ago. He works at a correctional institute in upstate New York and is the father of a handicapped son. He wrote an essay about how frustrating and disappointing his child had been, how he would often get angry at him and how embarrassing it was because the boy was always dropping things. One day they went to McDonald's, and the father was dreading being embarrassed in public once again by his son. At some point during the meal, he reached over and spilt his son's milk . . . and the boy handed him his napkin and said, 'It's okay, Daddy.' You can't possibly read this story and not weep.

The writer is no John Updike, but he had something very simple and beautiful to say and he did so with incredible honesty.

"I've done enough freelancing to know how tough it is, and some writers need more hand-holding than others, so I'll never penalize someone for being a nudge! However, there *is* one lethal combination: being a lousy writer who's also a pain in the neck. I've discovered that the ones who can't write their way out of a paper bag also tend to be the ones who call you forty times a week.

"At another magazine where I once worked there was one writer who was *tenacious*—he'd call four times a week. After it had been going on for a while, I finally had to tell him, 'You don't write well—in fact, your work will never meet our standards, and the kinds of stories you like to do we don't publish.' Even after *that* he had the chutzpah to call two weeks later to pitch an idea.

"The freelancers I most like to work with are those who not only write well but who also take criticism maturely. Most people, by the way, can't. I don't criticize capriciously, and I expect writers to take my comments seriously. I've dealt with writers who've said, 'Do whatever you want with my story!' But I'd rather they say, 'Send me your notes and I'll make the changes' or 'Let's work on this together.' A writer who can produce a good piece *and* revise a not-so-good piece is someone I'll work with any day.

"I also appreciate writers who *think* about the magazine and the reader, writers whose commitment to the magazine is demonstrated. For example, they'll send me a relevant newspaper clipping or a sample of *another* writer's work with a note saying, 'I thought he'd be great for *Parents* because I know you're looking for more essays from fathers.' I won't put a star next to that writer's name, but I'll remember her. If I meet you and I feel that you're a mensch, it helps. It tells me not only that I'll enjoy working with you but also that chances are the reader will like reading you too."

PARENTS, 685 Third Avenue, New York, NY 10017; (212) 878-8700.
Frequency of Publication: monthly.
Circulation: 1.725 million.
Readership: parents of children from birth to twelve years, but mostly eight and younger.
Available Upon Request: free writer's guidelines and sample copy.
Payment Rate: one dollar a word.

PETER BLOCH, EDITOR, *PENTHOUSE*

"I truly believe that the world doesn't need more freelance writers."

"Unlike a lot of other magazines, *Penthouse* has a wide-ranging audience, encompassing everyone from college students to Wall Street lawyers, from farmers to people working in Washington, from truck drivers to prisoners. We get mail from all these people. We also have women who read the magazine, although they don't buy it. For many readers, *Penthouse* and television are their main sources of information. There's a lot of populist feeling out there— for example, we've been doing stories on Vietnam vets since 1974, when a lot of people still viewed them as baby-killers. We've been there for them for a long time, and they know it.

"When it comes to writing for this magazine, if you're the greatest writer in the world, personality doesn't matter. I deal with a great number of writers whom I don't like personally—I just deal with them. I may curse you when I hang up the phone, but if you're good enough, you can get away with all kinds of things. What matter most are the quality of the writing and the quality of the work that goes into the writing.

"Here at *Penthouse* an unknown writer will not get through to me—or to any top editor—except by accident. Therefore, it's *very* important to be polite to my assistants—they control enormous power. And when you call, *tell* them what you're calling about. I'm annoyed by people who call and say, 'It's confidential—I'll only talk to Peter Bloch.' In those cases I never call back, and I tell my assistant to call and insist on knowing what it's about. It's very, very rare when someone's obtained the Pentagon Papers and *must* talk only to the top editor.

"A lot of people become freelance writers because they don't like the nine-to-five office routine. They're free spirits—they want to wake up when they want to wake up and write when they want to write—and that's fine. But we editors *do* have schedules, and we're not going to deal with writers when it's convenient for *them*.

"The mentality of many freelance writers is that the world revolves around *them*. When *they* want to speak with you, you should be available. 'I'm a writer, a *creative* person,' is the thinking. But writers must extend some courtesy to their editor. I hear freelancers say, 'I'm working on my novel, then I'm going out of town,' and when they get back they call and say, 'Here I am; let's meet for a drink.' (That means, Buy me a drink so I can get an advance.) But if I'm busy and can't get back to you for a week or two, you have to realize that's what makes the world go round. This is a *business*. Even if freelancers are choosing not to come into an office every day, it's still a business.

"Concentrate on being a *professional*. Many novice free-lancers read about hard-drinking, hard-living writers, but usually one thing is true: they don't screw around with their work. Professional writers are usually very professional. If I tell Harrison Salisbury I have to cut five hundred words from his piece to make it fit, he's fine about it, while a novice freelancer may become very upset if you change his semicolon to an ellipsis.

"Here's an example of something that came in today. This is a fax from a man whose name is vaguely familiar to me. He writes: 'You remember we spoke *last year* [italics added] on South African terrorism . . .' I probably told him to send me more. 'The proposal is still on the drawing board . . .' That probably means he looked into it, but it was too much work. 'Now I have another idea I want to discuss with you . . .' Imagine if *I* had waited a year to get back to *him*!

"I think I'm fair; I don't want to be high-handed with writers. Any publication wants to attract as many high-level writers, agents, and publishers as possible, and we're no exception. *Penthouse* pays well, but let's face it, we're controversial, so why add to the controversy by being obnoxious? I find that by being fair you usually get a writer's best work. I know a lot of writers who are badly treated by editors. Even if the magazine pays well and is prestigious, after a few times the writer may feel it's not worth it. I don't want writers to have that feeling here.

"The writer-editor relationship is unique—it's part personal, part professional. As friendly as the relationship may seem, bear in mind that it really *isn't* a friendship. If an editor is a professional, he'll occasionally have to say harsh things, and at that point the writer isn't his friend; he's someone the editor has contracted to do business with. Learn not to get easily hurt.

"I truly believe that the world doesn't need more freelance writers. I'd say that half of those who call themselves freelancers should get another job and stop fooling themselves. I once spoke at a writers' conference, and somebody got up and said, 'Bob Guccione [publisher of *Penthouse*] wouldn't be a millionaire if it weren't for us writers!' Yes, writers are important, but even so, I don't need to put up with individuals who are unprofessional in everything from their spelling to their attitude on the phone. Writers have asked me, 'What's to stop you from stealing my ideas?' If *that's* your approach, don't be a freelance writer. It's not that editors are such saints, but it's rare for anyone to have a unique idea. There are millions of good ideas out there.

"Writing is a very demanding profession. Just because you have an idea and can type on a computer doesn't mean others will agree you're a writer. A friend of mine asked me to speak to his writing class—the course was called How to Survive as a Freelance Writer in New York City. My presentation basically consisted of two words: 'Forget it!' I told them, 'You're *not* going to survive as a freelance writer! Don't give up your job, for God's sake! You don't have much to contribute. People like me employ people full-time to keep people like you away from me!' There are so many of those people out there. Every day they spend at a course like that is one day less spent perfecting their craft. If you love writing, you can probably achieve some success, but you won't necessarily reach the level of *Penthouse*."

PENTHOUSE, 1965 Broadway, New York, NY 10023; (212) 496-6100.
Frequency of Publication: monthly.
Circulation: 2.25 million.
Readership: men from eighteen to forty; all economic and social levels.
Available Upon Request: free writer's guidelines.
Payment Rate: one dollar a word minimum.

PATRICIA BISESTO, MANAGING EDITOR, *PLAYGIRL*

"If you lie about when the story will be in, it's over between us."

"*Playgirl* is a seventeen-year-old monthly magazine for women between eighteen and thirty-four, with the vast majority of them in their early- to mid-twenties. They tend to be high-school graduates with maybe one year of college, and they hold 'pink-collar' jobs—they're hairdressers, bank tellers, nurses. And, obviously, if they're reading *Playgirl*, they're more uninhibited than the average woman.

"The photos of nude men are naturally the magazine's most controversial aspect, but we know that our readers like them—for the nine or so months in 1987 when we did away with frontal nudity, readership plummeted. Now we're back up to six hundred thousand happy readers a month.

"The most important thing to remember about writing for *Playgirl* is that unlike most other women's magazines, we don't tell readers what's wrong with them—we try to focus on how to make the most of what and who they are. Therefore, we'll never publish an article on how to lose ten pounds; instead, we might run a fashion feature on clothes for larger-sized women. Rather than tell women how to stop being jealous, we'll do a story on how jealousy can actually make a relationship better.

"The best writers understand what we're trying to do editorially, but there are still plenty of writers who don't get it. Let me give you an example: I recently assigned a profile of KISS singer Paul Stanley to a writer I'd used before. She called me after the interview to tell me she'd spent two days with Paul, that he was fabulous, and that the interview would be great.

"What do I get from her? A bizarre manuscript that

gushed about Paul Stanley, that showed absolutely no objectivity, that had lines in it like, 'No, Paul Stanley *didn't* pay me to write this piece.' The article told us more about the writer than I cared to know, even more than about the subject. Furthermore, she was too lazy—or simply too taken with Paul—to do a good job on the writing, and instead of putting in proper transitions, she simply jumped from one thought to another, using subheads to break up the sections. When I asked her about this technique, she said something about it being 'cool.'

"As if all that weren't bad enough, when I told her the piece needed a rewrite, she gave me a really hard time about it—she kept trying to convince me that she'd given me what the readers wanted. She eventually did a rewrite, but it wasn't very good and I had to have one of my editors redo it. It was a terrible experience. I won't say that I'll never work with this writer again—she *has* done good stories for me in the past. But I realize those pieces were successful only because I'd given her *very* detailed instructions in my assignment letters. This time I was a little more casual about what I wanted and it backfired. I need to be very careful with this writer.

"What kind of writers make me happy? Someone like Rich Rober, who writes for the Chicago *Sun-Times* and does great humor pieces for 'The Men's Room,' one of our two humor columns. I discovered Rich's stuff in the slush pile—which is a way of saying you don't necessarily need to have a track record to break into *Playgirl;* you simply have to have a feel for the material.

"As for Rich, he originally sent me ten short articles, unsolicited. Of those ten I bought one, and now he does regular full-length features for me. He's a good writer who consistently comes up with great ideas. In the beginning I went over his material with him step by step, and he takes direction very well; in effect, I taught him how to write for

Playgirl. Now his copy comes in almost perfect—I barely touch it. It's so *nice* when somebody follows directions; so few do.

"Although I think our stories are pretty straightforward, I've been told by some writers that they find it difficult to write for a magazine that revolves around sex. There has to be some connection with either sex or relationships for a story to make sense for *Playgirl.* For example, we did an article on depression which discussed, for a paragraph or two, how depression affects one's sex life. There always needs to be that sexual angle.

"Another little pet peeve of mine: people who call the second after they send in a story. That drives me *crazy.* Even though I'm good about reading stuff quickly—usually right after it comes in—I still need time to collect my thoughts about it before I discuss it with a writer. Give me a week, at least. The same is true if you've sent in a query—wait a week, then call to remind me about it.

"And speaking of queries, *mail* them, don't call them in. Talking about ideas over the phone usually doesn't give me enough of a sense about the story, and it certainly doesn't tell me what your writing is like. Even if I like an idea over the phone, I'll still ask to see a couple of paragraphs. So save your time and mine by mailing your ideas.

"If you bug me for money every three minutes, I'm going to stop using you.

"And if you know you can't meet a deadline, ask for an extension. If you lie about when the story will be in, it's over between us. I'd rather hear that a story will be late than be lied to."

PLAYGIRL, 801 Second Avenue, New York, NY 10017; (212) 986-5100.
Frequency of Publication: monthly.

Circulation: 600,000
Readership: female from eighteen to thirty-four.
Available Upon Request: free writer's guidelines with an SASE.
Payment Rate: Thirty cents a word for the first few stories, more
later.

SUSAN LYNE, EDITOR, AND PETER BISKIND, EXECUTIVE EDITOR, *PREMIERE*

**"Our readers are people who find the inner
workings of the [movie] business sexy."**

"When we started *Premiere,* we found a large and growing audience of people not just interested in movies but in
the industry as well," says Lyne. "Usually what you see is
that a new Molly Ringwald movie comes out, and then a
piece about her appears that's essentially the same story
you've read a thousand times. But we're more than just
celebrity profiles. We've discovered readers who are interested in going beyond the fluff that passes for movie journalism. We wanted to create a magazine about the movie
business that would be journalistically sound and would
take the readers behind the scenes, too, showing them how
movies are made. Our readers are people who find the inner workings of the business sexy."

"*Premiere* caught on very quickly in the industry," adds
Biskind. "It is unique. Magazines like *Vanity Fair, Esquire,*
and *Rolling Stone* do their share of film articles, but there's
nothing else that has the format we have."

"A good way to break in," says Lyne, "is via one of our
departments. For example, 'Cameos'—brief profiles of hot
new actors, directors, producers, and others. 'Short Takes'
features movie-related newsbreaks and trivia. We don't

77

take a lot of stories over the transom—perhaps one piece per issue is from someone we've never worked with before. We started out strictly freelance, but we're using the staff to do more and more writing. For example, Peter Biskind wrote our recent cover story on Dustin Hoffman.

"We're good about responding to queries promptly, usually the week they come in, even when they're from writers we don't know. We receive about thirty a week. If you haven't heard back from us in about two weeks, you should call.

"We've managed to land some elusive subjects, such as Hoffman and Steven Spielberg. If we've done a significant profile of you in *Premiere,* it's considered a mark of recognition that you're an important player in the industry."

Adds Biskind, "Of course, there's still a group of publicists who'll flip out over a negative item about their people. But, in general, they understand that we don't 'go after' people; we treat them fairly. If there is some criticism, it's usually balanced with something positive. They're not afraid we're going to eviscerate them like, say, *Spy* magazine."

"Do we get into celebrities' personal lives? Only if it affects the work they do," says Lyne. "For example, we recently did a story on Sam Kinison, the controversial stand-up comic, and it talked in part about his drug use and how he abused people; the article dealt with the way that behavior destroyed his film career. Our readers thought the story was appropriate for *Premiere.*

"We tend to assign West Coast stories to West Coast writers and East Coast stories to East Coast writers, with rare exception. If you're looking for an expenses-paid, cross-country trip to write a piece for us, it isn't likely to happen. But, for instance, if you live in Memphis and know about a movie being shot there, we may have you cover the story. That might be a time we're willing to take a risk with a writer we don't know.

"If you don't already specialize in Hollywood stories,

that's not a problem. We constantly try to bring in people who aren't necessarily known as entertainment writers, people we think are good general reporters and who can bring a fresh eye to the subject. One of them is Teresa Carpenter, a Pulitzer Prize–winning journalist whose writing specialty is homicide."

"Plan ahead—six months in advance, if possible," says Biskind. "If an article is pegged to an upcoming movie, the piece will come out when the movie comes out. We're hostage to a movie's release schedule. In that respect, unlike other magazines, we're not totally in command of our own table of contents."

"Spend time reading *Premiere*," Lyne urges. "There's a style and tone to it. Occasionally a query pops out at us. There's a smart person behind it, someone who's really thought about the story he's pitching to us."

PREMIERE, 2 Park Avenue, New York, NY 10016; (212) 725-4200.
Frequency of Publication: monthly.
Circulation: 400,000.
Readership: 50 percent men, 50 percent women.
Available Upon Request: free writer's guidelines.
Payment Rate: one dollar a word minimum.

CLELL BRYANT, SENIOR EDITOR, *READER'S DIGEST*

"A writer with a good personality—a great 'salesperson'—may manage to get an assignment where a shy person may not."

"One civilized thing freelance writers discover when dealing with *Reader's Digest:* there are no form rejection slips. Anyone writing to an editor gets a personal reply, even with all the mail we get. (The *Digest* receives thousands of letters a month.) If, for example, I see that someone is a professional freelancer, I will reply personally, just out of courtesy. And, of course, if there's a glimmer of promise there or it's a natural-born story for the *Digest,* one jumps upon it with glee.

"If the person isn't a professional writer and offers an idea that is patently unsuitable, I will send it on to our Editorial Correspondence Department, headed by Elinor Griffith. Mail sent to no particular editor ends up in that department, too, and the people who work for Elinor are alert to stories with possibilities. Anything with potential is sent to an interested editor. I am one of about fifty, and of those there are about twenty of us who might look at queries that have been screened.

"I develop stories for the magazine's thirty-eight international editions as well as for the U.S. edition. I'm still finding new writers all the time, but someone really has to be exceptional for me to want to add him or her to those with whom I'm already working. *Reader's Digest* can afford to be picky—we pay top rates and have a circulation of 16.25 million in this country alone, with about 100 million readers worldwide.

"What makes writers good? They *deliver.* They're hardworking, talented, and highly amenable to taking direction. They're quick to understand what we want, that the *Digest* is special and more demanding than other magazines. We want stories done in a particular way, incorporating more research and more anecdotes. More work goes into a typical *Digest* story than one of comparable length in other magazines.

"The best writers pour their hearts into these pieces. They're highly professional. More often than not we ask for revisions, and our writers are very professional about doing them. Above all, a *Digest* contributor is an excellent *writer*. By the time the manuscript comes in and is seen by me and my colleagues, it stands or falls on its own. Of course, a writer with a good personality—a great 'salesperson'—may manage to get an assignment where a shy person may not. Still, it's what's on paper that counts in the end.

"There's no doubt about it: it's tough breaking in to the *Digest*. A writer may need to do two to three versions of an outline to get it just right, before it can go to our editor-in-chief, Ken Gilmore. Quite frequently outlines are turned down—I'd say fewer than half make it to the assignment stage. As for completed manuscripts that come over the transom, a very small number of them ever see the light of day. Our editorial correspondents are not even supposed to read unsolicited manuscripts. (They do read story proposals and published articles for possible reprint.)

"But difficult as it is to sell to us, we'll go a long way with a writer with a good idea. There are so many demands and parameters on a typical story, and so many elements must be exactly right, that we'll work for a long time with a writer who is able to deliver.

"Recently a teenager living in North Carolina sent in a story intended as a 'Drama in Real Life,' telling how she and two friends attending language school in Switzerland had gotten lost on a mountain. A smart person in the Editorial Correspondence Department spotted it and told her the story didn't work as a 'Drama in Real Life,' because she was giving away the ending by telling it in the first person. So the editorial correspondent suggested that if the writer redid it in the third person and got the story published locally, the *Digest* might consider it as a possible pickup. The teenager, working this time with a local journalist, revised the story and got it published in North Carolina, in the *Yadkin Ripple.* They reworked it again for me, giving the story more drama, and now the piece will run in several of our foreign editions.

"This girl was only fifteen or so, and I was extremely impressed by her. It was clear she read my letter very carefully and revised the story exactly as I had outlined. What irritates me is when a writer reads my letter and then ignores it.

"To whom should you send your manuscript? If you know the name of a particular editor, you could mail it to that person, but if you don't, you can address it to our assistant managing editor, Phil Osborne. Only great stories, ones that get to the reader's emotions, are accepted. Such a story won't get lost at the *Digest.*

"The standard 'entry-level' payment for a story for the U.S. edition of *Reader's Digest* is three thousand dollars. That's for about four thousand words, which we then cut to twenty-five hundred or so. We like to work that way because even the best writers use excess verbiage. Also, if they are trying to write to length, they might omit a good anecdote or fact—once writers start editing themselves, something important might be lost. After you've done a few stories for the *Digest,* the pay rates go up and are negotiated individually by your sponsoring editor. We apply to the editor-in-chief for a boost in rates for the writer.

"*Reader's Digest* was first published in 1922, and in sixty-eight years we've never lost the foundation of solid journalism that reaches people and helps them in their daily lives. If we've changed at all, it's that we've become more contemporary—we try to stay on the edge of the news. And more than ever before, we're looking for elements that touch the reader's emotions."

READER'S DIGEST, Pleasantville, NY 10570; (914) 238-1000.
Frequency of Publication: monthly.

Circulation: 16.25 million (U.S. edition).
Readership: 58 percent women, 42 percent men; median age forty-five.
Available Upon Request: free writer's guidelines.
Payment Rate: a minimum of three thousand dollars for four thousand words.

STEVEN REDDICLIFFE, ASSOCIATE EDITOR, *SELF*

**"This isn't forced labor; we want writers to
be enthusiastic about the assignments we give
them."**

"What kind of writers do I think are good? To begin with, those who send their query addressed to the right person at the magazine. It sounds simple, but it's a clear indication of a writer's interest and attention to detail. It's annoying to an editor to receive a proposal addressed to someone who hasn't been here for two or three years.

"A freelancer's query letter or a phone query should demonstrate a real working knowledge of the magazine. It's essential that a writer subscribe to the publication or, at the very least, go to the library and study six recent issues. Doing that tells you what we've already done, as well as gives you good ideas for what we're looking for. For example, if somebody were to read our 'Moneywise' column on buying a first house, she might get an idea to do a story on how to upgrade one's current house to make it more valuable. That sort of understanding comes from reading the magazine.

"When we get letters addressed to the wrong people or on a topic we covered three issues ago, I think it reflects a basic laziness on the part of the freelancer. When an editor decides to assign a piece, he or she wants to give it to someone sharper than that. This sort of thing is usually found among inexperienced writers.

"Potential writers for *Self* should know that we're still primarily a health magazine but that we've become a total *lifestyle* magazine for women. Health, nutrition, and fitness continue to constitute our main focus, but we've expanded to include fashion, more beauty than ever before, more on money and careers, and a larger number of general features. And while we're not a celebrity magazine, we *have* featured personalities such as Amanda Pays and Courtney Cox on our covers and have run features on people like Meg Ryan and Carey Lowell, whose lifestyles are of interest to *Self*'s readers.

"We really stress *reporting* at *Self*—our stories are thoroughly researched and reported. We look for writers who know whom to call on a given subject. The best writers can just pick up the phone and interview a good number of people for useful quotes that support the writers' contentions. For a piece of 1000 words or longer, you need to talk to *several* sources. Poorly reported stories are disappointing. If a 1500-word piece comes in with only two sources quoted, it indicates that not a lot of work has been put into it, even though there might be a lot of *thought* in it.

"It's also okay to ask if we have people who'd be good to quote—we usually have names to start the writer off with. Editors here try to do a great deal of research themselves—we read many magazines and newspapers—and if someone has something interesting to say on a topic we've assigned, we'll send a photocopy of the article to the writer. *Self* has always been known for the solidness of its health and fitness reporting, and that terrific reporting is still one of our hallmarks.

"Along with health, we're also seeking good *lifestyle* reporting—current issues affecting women's lives. We recently ran a piece on nontraditional marriages: commuter marriages, relationships where the wife works and the husband stays at home, and so on. In addition, we want stories on the 'new American family,' that is, different combinations of people living together, such as a father and son, or three unrelated people.

"We look for writers from all over the country, especially newspaper reporters. In recent months we've used quite a few newspaper writers. We like them a lot; people who've done that kind of writing tend to have good reporting ability.

"One thing that makes editors unhappy is when a writer is late on a story and hasn't bothered to say why. Any number of times we've had to track down writers two to four weeks after the story was due to say, 'Hey, what's doing?' I realize there's often a good reason for the delay, such as family problems—it happens to everybody. But it's smart to call and say, 'I'm going to be late' or 'I'm having trouble and here's why.' It's rare for an editor *not* to give extra time if the writer needs it, and it's unprofessional if the editor has to track you down. Often, these are the very writers who are the first to call about their check. It's just a matter of being responsible. We're not a bunch of tough guys. All I'm talking about here is exhibiting common courtesy, a good idea in *any* business.

"Once I assigned a story to a writer, and at some point he called to say he had messengered it over to our office. We never got it, and I told him so. He then claimed he had messengered it a *second* time, but we never got *that* either. Then the writer disappeared! We never saw the piece or heard from him again—although I kept seeing his byline in other magazines. I don't understand what happened. Maybe he couldn't do the piece and was simply too embarrassed to say so, but editors won't hold a grudge if a story turns out to be something a writer doesn't want to do. This isn't forced labor; we want writers to be enthusiastic about the assignments we give them.

"Our payment rates are very good—I've never heard anybody complain about their being too low. And Condé Nast [which owns *Self*] pays quickly, so people don't complain about slow payment either. If you're a first-time writer for us, we'll offer a reasonable fee for the first manuscript and might consider a higher rate the next time. We listen to writers' requests about money and try to make them happy as best we can."

SELF, 350 Madison Avenue, New York, NY 10017; (212) 880-8800.
Frequency of Publication: monthly.
Circulation: 1.2 million.
Readership: Working women; median age twenty-nine; half are single, half are married.
Available Upon Request: free writer's guidelines.
Payment Rate: one dollar a word minimum.

ROBERTA ANNE MYERS, ARTICLES EDITOR, *SEVENTEEN*

"If someone's a mediocre writer *and* annoying, why bother?"

"There are more teenage magazines out there than ever before, but there are real differences. *Sassy* has a completely different voice from ours. *YM,* which has recently been redesigned, used to be narrower, more 'girly' than *Seventeen.* I feel that of the three, we're the only one doing real journalism. And we've been trying to be more aggressive lately about getting 'name' writers into the magazine—and they respond! Sometimes we're so surprised when they say yes, but it's because of *Seventeen*'s reputation and the fact that the magazine holds some fascination for them.

"Two years ago the magazine was bought by Rupert Murdoch. Our standards are as high as ever, but there have been some changes editorially. For instance, we've added more pages on careers and travel. We've also refocused our food pages to encompass living and style, and our entertainment pieces, which were once totally staff-written, are now about two-thirds freelance.

"Writing for *Seventeen* isn't easy—getting freelancers who don't preach is difficult. The writers we always turn to are ones whose voice is absolutely right for *Seventeen,* who have an obvious understanding of the issues and of a teenager's point of view.

"A lot of writers send us queries that make us ask ourselves, 'Have you *ever* picked up the magazine?' Often it seems as though they've never even looked at it. For example, I got a query the other day from a woman who wanted to write about watching her teenage daughter grow up, get married, and have children. *Seventeen* is not the place for a story like that. *Maybe* we'd consider something about grandmothers and granddaughters, but not this sort of reminiscence—it's really for older readers. It's actually a little insulting when a writer asks you for your time when she hasn't taken time herself to research the magazine.

"Another problem in writing for us is that a lot of people just don't have much day-to-day contact with teenagers. These writers may *think* they understand young people, but they really don't know what's happening—and that's reflected in their proposals. Think in terms of a *teenager's* schedule. A kid's life is pegged to the school year, so it's silly to suggest a story on how to apply to college for our summer issues. Know the lead time of a magazine—at *Seventeen* we plan three to six months in advance.

"My feeling about dealing with writers' personalities is: if they can write, they're worth putting up with, but if they can only *sort of* write, then they may or may not be worth putting up with. During our story meetings someone might say, 'Let's assign it to———,' and someone else will say, 'Oh, he's a pain in the neck.' If someone's a mediocre writer *and* annoying, why bother?

"Last year I worked with one writer who was unbelievable. He called about writing for us, and he submitted his clips and several ideas. About ten days went by, then I called him to apologize about the delay and to say that his clips were good but his ideas weren't quite right. He exploded! He screamed, 'You editors think you control the world! I made a hundred thousand dollars last year! I earn three times what you do!' I was more fascinated than upset—it was clear to me that something was really wrong with him.

"He called me the next day to apologize. He said, 'I'm really sorry I lost my temper, but I've had a hard time lately with certain editors.' Since then I've talked to other editors who've dealt with him and they've all said, 'Oh, *him*! He's *nuts*!'

"That's an extreme example, of course, but I've had problems with other writers. For one thing, I'm not eager to work with people who've written one or two pieces for the magazine and who say when they're asked to do revisions, 'You're wrong! You don't know what I'm trying to do!' You have to be willing to do what's best for the magazine, and that might include having your 'voice' toyed with a little bit. I'm also reluctant to work with anyone who's difficult about completing the job. A few freelancers take on an assignment, thinking, It's only *Seventeen*—it's not *Vanity Fair* or *Rolling Stone*. So they'll turn in first drafts, and leave holes in their story that seem very obvious to us. That sort of thing isn't a personality flaw as much as just being lazy.

"Other writers get insulted if you ask them to submit clips; they want you to take them at their word about where they've been published. Again, I think it's that old 'It's only *Seventeen*' mentality. But I need to see how their writing will translate to *Seventeen*—*if* it will translate. It doesn't always, no matter how good a writer you may be.

"The writing—the work—is foremost for us when dealing with writers. The best ones tend to come back and work with us again and again—they seem to really like writing for *Seventeen*. I've found that people who want to show off to their friends don't write for us. Those who write for us do so because they *enjoy* writing for us, not because they think it'll get them invited to good parties.

"Generally speaking, I think we treat writers pretty well. Everybody here really cares about the magazine—at some other magazine, editors care more about their own careers than the publication. Much of our concern has to do with the readers. They love us! They write us letters saying things like, 'My boyfriend was beating me up and I didn't know what to do. You saved my life.' It's pretty rewarding."

SEVENTEEN, 850 Third Avenue, New York, NY 10022; (212) 759-8100.
Frequency of Publication: monthly.
Circulation: 1.75 million.
Readership: Young women fourteen to twenty-one; median age fifteen.
Available Upon Request: free writer's guidelines.
Payment Rate: one dollar a word.

MIKE SCHWANZ, SENIOR ASSOCIATE EDITOR,
SPORTS AFIELD

**"There have been writers who've shown up
in the lobby asking for me. I *don't* like
surprises like that!"**

"*Sports Afield* has been around since 1887. It's primarily
a magazine about hunting and fishing, but in recent years
it's become more broad based. We've run stories on everything from the phenomenon of thunderstorms to spiders to
killer bees to Lyme disease—just about anything that is of
interest in the world of the outdoors.

"We've done a repositioning of the magazine to make it
more service oriented than ever before, featuring more
how-to articles and fewer first-person narratives. Of course,
we're keeping the most successful things, such as the reproductions of wildlife art—that's very popular—and our best-
selling grizzly-bear cover, which is *Sports Afield*'s equiv-
alent of *Sports Illustrated*'s annual swimsuit issue.

"My biggest problem with freelancers is that they don't
study the magazine as they should. I'd say that 50 percent of
our queries come from writers who have no idea what *Sports
Afield* is about. You can tell that they've gone through some
magazine directory and stopped when they got to the word
sports. That's why we get queries about stories on the World
Cup Soccer Matches or Mats Wilander—you know these
writers have never seen *Sports Afield* in their life.

"Not only should writers be looking at recent issues of
the magazine, but it's also a good idea if they photocopy
the contents pages from several issues, to get a better sense
of what we've published. That way writers will see that if
we did a piece on deer hunting *in Arkansas,* we may not do
another one like it for five years, although we *do* cover
deer hunting on a regular basis.

"Given that fact, I'm always impressed by a freelancer who writes me a letter saying, 'I know you haven't done a story on caribou hunting since October 1985, but because the caribou population in Quebec has doubled in the last few years . . .' If you clearly demonstrate in your query that you read the magazine and then can knock me over with hard statistics, you'll get my attention. That's happened several times. It proves to me that you have a solid work ethic, that you're ambitious enough to go to the trouble of finding out this stuff.

"I'd say you should probably subscribe to all three major outdoor magazines—ours, *Outdoor Life,* and *Field and Stream;* it's cheap enough to do so. Those grizzled writers who are most successful in this field know what's going on in all three publications.

"Some writers come to us via a literary agent. We at *Sports Afield* view that as an attempt by the writer to look important. Agents are generally *book* people and not that familiar with magazine publishing. Therefore, the writer is introducing a third party who may not know the field at all. Freelancers are better off handling their own magazine work.

"Some writers tend to rule us out as a potential market— a freelancer who, say, works regularly for women's magazines probably couldn't do a piece on the best guns for squirrel hunting. However, if you look at the magazine you'll see we cover some subjects you might not expect. For instance, we'll do occasional stories on cooking (fish and animals you've caught), and we've done articles on getting physically fit in preparation for a hunting trip. In the future we'll also be increasing our product coverage, so you could conceivably do a roundup on the best cookstoves or tents. If you're creative, you can probably come up with a salable idea for us.

"What many people don't realize is that this magazine isn't just a useful guide for outdoors people; it's also extremely well written and edited. During the 1980s we've been nominated for more than a half-dozen National Magazine Awards, and we won in 1987. We were the only publication in our field to be nominated, much less win. Fortunately we have a number of terrific writers who make it possible. For example, last year we were nominated for our An American Classic series, which deals with different aspects of hunting and fishing. The writer of the series, Tony Atwill, is not some Nazi-like fanatic who likes to shoot at everything he sees; he's a great writer with a good sense of humor about the subject. He's also very easy to work with.

"I love when writers make it easy for me. For instance, I appreciate it when they make a point of telling me where they are and when. Our contributors are away on trips much of the time, often to very remote parts of the world, and I've lost ten years of my life trying to track down writers who may be in Africa for two weeks. It's so helpful if you let me know in a cover note, 'I'll be at the following number July 1–14, but then I'll be out of the country for . . .' I think fondly of any writer who remembers to do things like that.

"My policy on taking writers to lunch is the following: if anyone has contributed to the magazine, especially our better and longtime writers, I'll take him out when he comes to New York. If a writer is making an effort to see us, we *like* to meet with him personally to discuss things. If you plan ahead and drop me a letter telling me when you'll be in New York, I'll be glad to have lunch with you. Then, again, there have been writers who've shown up in the lobby asking for me—I *don't* like surprises like that!

"The magazine is very graphics oriented, and about half the stories require that the author take his own photographs. After all, if you're doing a piece about big-sheep hunting in British Columbia and you're at the top of a ten-thousand-foot mountain, we're depending on you to come back with good-quality, 35mm slides. Ours is one of the few areas of journalism left where writers have to be photographers too. If you're a mediocre writer and a great outdoor photographer, you'll have a far better chance with *Sports Afield* than if the opposite were true.

"This field used to attract some great writers—Zane Grey, Ernest Hemingway. We at *Sports Afield* don't expect brilliant, Hemingwayesque writing. The main requirement is to be able to produce an informative, well-organized story that flows well, so that someone sitting in his armchair at home can easily picture what's being described. It sounds simple—but it really isn't, of course."

SPORTS AFIELD, 250 West 55th Street, New York, NY 10019; (212) 649-2000.
Frequency of Publication: monthly.
Circulation: 530,000.
Readership: men; median age 36.4.
Available Upon Request: free writer's guidelines.
Payment Rate: approximately seventy-five cents a word.

JANEL BLADOW, FEATURES EDITOR, *THE STAR*

"I . . . get annoyed by writers who begin bellyaching about money even before they do the assignment."

"My biggest gripe about writers is laziness. It really shocks me. They're supposed to be professionals! We're real detail oriented at *The Star*—we look for every detail you can imagine—and then we get stories from freelancers that just *skim* the surface. The writers give me the crud off the top instead of the meat inside. It's very irritating, and yet they are appalled when they're asked to do a rewrite.

"I recently gave an assignment to a woman, and I told her very specifically what I wanted: a piece about Wall Street types who had been hippies in the sixties. What did I get? A story about people who are hippies *now*. She also submitted the highest bill I'd ever gotten from a freelancer for a story. (I *did* tell her I'd pay her more if the story were really good, but obviously it wasn't.) She didn't even work that hard on it—it was clear she had talked to just a couple of friends of friends. As it happens, *I* had once done a similar story for *Working Woman*. I remember calling every brokerage house in New York City, interviewing anyone who'd ever been a sixties hippie. I found the people I needed for the story, but I'd spent *days* doing the research. My writer at *The Star* didn't.

"I also get annoyed by writers who begin bellyaching about money even before they do the assignment. I don't understand it! After all, these writers *want* the assignment and know roughly what we pay. We pay the going rate; in fact, we pay *better* than most newspapers for feature stories. This is quick turnaround stuff—we're really a cross between a newspaper and a magazine. And I *do* try to be fair to writers—someday I may want to work for *them*! But many of them still complain constantly. If I have a piece of advice, it's this: Don't whine! Be professional! Tell me the story, get the assignment, do the job, and let me know how it's progressing. If we can keep it all up front, then nobody will feel bad about anything.

"Another complaint I have: writers who don't read the publication they're submitting to. It's important to study the market and adjust your style and ideas to the audience for which you're writing. We get tons of submissions and often I wonder, Is this person just sending this out to every magazine on the off chance *someone* will buy it? All I have to do is open my mail on any given day and I'll find wildly inappropriate submissions.

"Here's one: 'Fear Not Friday the 13th!' We haven't done a story on the number thirteen in . . . thirteen years! Here's another one: 'The Story Behind Your Hotel Bible'—why there's a Bible in your hotel room. This writer has *no* idea what my magazine is publishing. There's no way in the *world* we'd run a story like that!

"What we're looking for are stories that are lively, unusual, interesting, and newsworthy. We're not just a celebrity magazine; we also do general-interest pieces, pop psychology, and trend stories. We use a lot of freelance material each week—I'd say I work with about twenty freelancers on a regular basis. As for how we get our ideas, many come off the top of our head, as well as from reading lots of newspapers—we subscribe to papers from all over the country. In fact, because we do so many regional stories, a freelancer in Laredo, Texas, for instance, has a better chance of selling me an idea than someone here in New York.

"One of my best writers lives in Portland, Oregon. Recently he went through his local papers and found a story about a little boy who'd been lost in the woods for three days, with his dogs keeping him warm. Our executive editors happened to be desperate for a human-interest story that week, so the writer got the assignment. In the meantime, the Green River [Oregon] Murderer—the serial killer who killed forty women—had been found, and one woman came forward saying she had lived in his basement for a year. How incredible! 'I Lived with the Green River Murderer!' We wanted the story right away, before the thundering herd of journalists got to her. So we assigned that story to the same Portland writer.

"If you have breaking news and it's a really good story, call me. If it's a good story that's *not* making national headlines, send me a copy of the newspaper clip and tell me a bit about yourself and why you're qualified to write the piece. Our lead time on breaking stories is a week; on other features, it can be up to a month.

"I'm also looking for well-written, atmospheric interviews with big-name celebrities. These pieces are always on spec—I'll tell the writers, 'Okay, try it,' because we're not always sure they can get the story. Not every celebrity wants to be interviewed for *The Star,* and some writers won't mention who the story is for to the publicist. Other times, writers will spin off material from other interviews. For example, I may see a celebrity profile I like in *Good Housekeeping* or *Redbook,* and I'll contact the writer. She'll usually have extra information and will write a new story for me. I also don't mind getting good celeb pieces that were originally done for overseas markets. I have one guy in California who does celebrity interviews constantly, and he sells them to the U.K. and other countries. He's so well-known in California that he can get the interviews. I've bought a lot of his stuff, and we have an arrangement that he won't resell it in the U.S. until after I've run it.

"I'm always happy to have more good freelance writers, but understand the publication! And don't send me any more Friday the 13th stories!"

THE STAR, 660 White Plains Road, Tarrytown, NY 10591; (914) 332-5000.
Frequency of Publication: weekly.
Circulation: 3.5 million.
Readership: primarily female; average age thirty.
Available Upon Request: free writer's guidelines and sample copy.
Payment Rate: fifty cents a word.

DUNCAN MAXWELL ANDERSON, SENIOR EDITOR,
SUCCESS

**"It's your ass that's on the line. It's up to
you to be prudent."**

"*Success* is a business and management magazine that deals with ideas and disciplines. That means we often hear from people who know how to manage their business, or how to consult, or have terrific ideas for running a company—but can't write. In some cases they know how to do *none* of the above, but more often than not the person who approaches us with a story is someone with good ideas who doesn't know how to present them effectively on paper.

"Sometimes this businessman will hire someone to do the writing for him. So you get a lot of poor PR writers who think that by hooking up with this entrepreneur and writing under his byline, they're moving into real journalism. But generally what happens is that you get a combination of an inexperienced twenty-three-year-old with a businessman who wants to promote himself *without* giving away his secrets.

"What is the moral of all this for a potential *Success* writer? Don't be a ghostwriter if you notice that the guy isn't fond of giving his ideas away, doesn't have the spirit of throwing his bread upon the water, or is boring. Listen to your gut—and forget it. If you *must* work with someone, look for a person with good ideas who is willing to reveal them. He *will* get published, and you'll get some experience. Otherwise, you may find yourself in the untenable position of having to protect the businessman's ideas while writing a piece that's too bland for us to use. You have to try to shake the best stuff out of this egomaniac, and even when he won't give it to you, he'll still expect you to be able to place the story. Real egomania is impossible to work with.

"Another thing: make sure you're philosophically in sync with the subject you're writing about. We recently assigned a major story to a good, well-known writer who didn't particularly like entrepreneurship or business. I understand that many writers—especially male writers in their twenties with their testosterone racing—feel that they stand for the Truth. There's a big Sam Donaldson instinct in them, and I can relate to that; I was a freelance writer myself once.

"But to be successful in your business—and a freelance writer is a businessman or businesswoman with a completely unrelated talent for putting words together in a concise, exciting way—you must adapt your work to your market and be able to empathize with your reader's way of life. A young writer in Greenwich Village, for example, may not have much in common with a businessman in Illinois with a bushing factory. A guy running a business has certain values, certain things that are important to him. If you can't relate to them, learn to sympathize with them—it may make you a better writer. If you can't sympathize with them, find a different outlet for your writing.

"*Success* is not about the *people* who run businesses but about their *ideas* on running businesses—that's a subtle point that escapes many writers and PR reps. A freelancer hears about someone with an interesting and successful company, and the temptation is to write about the *personality* of the mogul in question. That's an approach *People* magazine would take, but not us. We don't care about people as people—our first priority is their secrets of business success. That's what we want to present to our readers. We supply them with ideas, as weapons and as inspiration.

"Therefore, to write for *Success* it's not enough simply to locate someone who runs an exciting company; you must look closely into his operation. For example, if you hear about a guy who made $200 million last year because his people are so well trained, pitch a story about his training system, *not* about his personality or his financial success. As far as we're concerned, the story has only done its job when it delivers to the readers the guy's ideas.

"I strongly urge freelance writers to get access to the editor-in-chief of any magazine they want to write for. Freelancing is a sales job. As with any sales job, it's smart to broaden your contacts and strengthen your relationships with key people. It's okay to be a bit of a pest. Show up at the office. Meet people. As a salesman trying to sell a story, you need to meet everyone who's in a position to say no. Get to know all the potential deal-killers and neutralize them.

"You also want to get as much information about the assignment as possible. If you're not completely clear about an assignment and the story doesn't work out, you wind up with a 20 percent kill fee while your editor risks nothing. When you get a go-ahead from a magazine, it's *you* who are taking the biggest risk; it's your ass that's on the line. It's up to you to be prudent. So meet the editor-in-chief if at all possible, and get *his* input and support. And if your assigning editor is touchy about your meeting his boss, run.

"I believe personal politics are very important in the word game—writing is not as market-driven as other businesses. It all comes down to relationships. Be friendly. Don't shrink from the chance to meet new people—CEOs of large corporations are often very ordinary, accessible men who like to talk. Writers who take the opportunity to meet people are those who win the game. I've seen it again and again."

SUCCESS, 342 Madison Avenue, New York, NY 10173; (212) 503-0700.

Frequency of Publication: monthly.

Circulation: 450,000.

Readership: 80 percent male, average age thirty-nine; 43 percent run their own business.

Available Upon Request: free writer's guidelines and sample copy.

Payment Rate: seventy-five cents to one dollar a word.

PAMELA FIORI, EDITORIAL DIRECTOR, *TRAVEL & LEISURE*

"Unless somebody has been knighted, I wouldn't dream of calling him 'sir.' We want a very eye-level relationship with writers."

"What makes writers delightful or awful to work with? Actually, I don't *care* what makes them one or the other; that's something for their shrink to deal with. But if a writer is truly difficult, I don't want to work with him or her. I can't *think* of a writer, even if he's written best-selling books, whose work justifies going through that kind of agony.

"At *Travel & Leisure* we are realistic in our opinion of writers: we don't revere them, but we do respect them. Unless somebody has been knighted, I wouldn't dream of calling him 'sir.' We want a very eye-level relationship with writers, with the understanding that we're each trying to do good for the other.

"We care about writers—we want their pieces to work and we want the writers themselves to succeed. So we never say, 'Write about anything you like.' *That* gives them license to fail. I don't know any writers who don't appreciate direction—direction means attention. I believe the

writer and the editor are *collaborating,* coming up with
something that's right for this particular magazine and no
other.

"There will always be writers who are insecure—in a
sense, their insecurity is a given. Editors have company,
but writers work in isolation, and they're dying to hear
from us as soon as possible. Still, some writers are much
more insecure than others.

"For example, we once gave a big assignment to a
writer—her job was to do a story about what it was like to
travel up and down the east coast of Florida. She must have
called me from a phone booth every two hours—'I'm in
Pompano Beach. Now what should I do?' Of course, I
don't mind an occasional phone call, especially if a place
isn't what I expected. But this writer needed so much hand-
holding that I began to lose faith in her, to doubt that she
could carry off the assignment. When we sent her down
there, we wanted her, in a sense, to pretend that she was
one of our readers—and we don't want insecure readers.
We want our writers to be grown-up and confident.

"Another writer who *was* confident—and a pleasure to
work with—was the late Joseph Wechsberg, who was based
in Vienna. He was about forty years older than I when we
first worked together, and he had written many wonderful
books and articles. I assigned him a piece on Vienna, but it
wasn't right—it needed a lot of work. Frankly, I was nervous about contacting him. I thought, I can permit him to
write a piece that I think is inferior and that won't be good
for either his reputation or ours, or I can take the chance
he'll be furious and refuse to do a rewrite and we'll have no
story, or he'll be agreeable. Finally I decided to write him,
telling him exactly what was wrong. He handed in his revision along with a note that said: 'Dear Miss Fiori, Thank
you for helping me. You know how to get a writer out of a
tunnel.' I still have that note.

"Even after all these years as an editor, it's so hard for me to have to ask for revisions, but I do it all the time. I guess some editors relish it, but I don't think any editor on my staff does. None of us wants to treat the writer as an adversary. So we try to guide him or her gently through the changes. I'm a writer myself, and while I don't like revising either, I'm always prepared for it. The monthly column I write in *Travel & Leisure* is read by my managing editor and executive editor, as well as by the editor of *Food & Wine*, with whom I've worked for years. Their job when reading my work is the same as when they read *any* contributor's work: don't allow the writer to sound like a fool. *Travel & Leisure* is the leader in its field, and we have to have a strong tone of authority. If we sound naive or oversimplify something, it not only reflects on the writer but also on the magazine.

"Many writers want to work for us because they enjoy traveling, and frequently they have the opportunity to take press trips [paid for by a government tourist office, a hotel, etc.]. But several years ago we stopped accepting junkets or assigning stories to writers who took them. *Travel & Leisure* pays all expenses now—and they can be sizable—so we have to be careful, especially with major pieces. No one on the staff takes free trips anymore either. So while it's bye-bye to those long weekends in Paris and those five-day jaunts to Hong Kong, our editors are forced to travel more selectively and to those places we can get more out of. It lets them—as well as our freelance writers—plan their *own* trip, without being accompanied by press people. As a result, they're traveling as our readers would.

"The best way for a new writer to start working for us is to write for one of our six regional sections, which appear in issues distributed to certain parts of the U.S. and not others. We pay less for these pieces—they're shorter and more specific to one area of the country—but it's a nice tryout for a freelancer, and we've promoted lots of writers from writing regional to national stories. Or come up with an essay for the front or back of the book.

"Read the magazine; there are no secrets about what we want. The worst thing a writer could say is, 'I'm going to———. Are you interested in a piece?' We won't send someone on a Caribbean vacation for two weeks at our expense. We're demanding, and we take all assignments very seriously. Any article we run must be *valid;* that is, it must influence the reader in some way, by leading him to a specific place or by changing his attitude about the way he wanders the world. It won't happen with every piece or with every issue, of course, but we do strive to make our readers better travelers. And if they're armchair travelers, we'd like to get them *out* of that chair."

TRAVEL & LEISURE, 1120 Avenue of the Americas, New York, NY 10036; (212) 382-5600.
Frequency of Publication: monthly.
Circulation: 1.1 million.
Readership: 50 percent male, 50 percent female; median age forty-eight.
Payment Rate: one dollar a word.

MYLES CALLUM, SENIOR EDITOR, *TV GUIDE*

"Recently we received a piece we assigned a year and a half ago!"

"I started out as a freelancer, and I'm impressed by anybody who tries to do it and is a success. Generally speaking, I've found freelancers to be good and bright and interesting people who want to please the editor because writing for magazines is their livelihood. In the scheme of things, freelancers are not high on my list of complaints in life.

"But there *was* a recent incident involving a writer that bothered me. She submitted a story proposal, which was then discussed at an editorial conference. Three days later I sent her a letter, which was prompt and courteous, giving several reasons why the idea wasn't right for *TV Guide.* I thought that was that—but no! The writer sent me back another letter, telling me why we were missing the boat and invoking the names of Walter Annenberg [the founder of *TV Guide*] and Rupert Murdoch [the owner]. Needless to say, this *isn't* the way to win friends among editors.

"This was, admittedly, an unusual episode. A more frequent problem is with query letters—most writers don't know how to write them. Many are too long and too diffuse; they're turnoffs from the word *go.* They should be short, lively, and punchy. If you can't put your idea across in two or three paragraphs, you may not have your story yet. If we want to hear more, we'll ask for a more detailed pitch later on.

"Another habit that bugs me is when a writer sends in a piece or a query and calls me about it the day I get it. He'll call on the pretext that he's just making sure the query was received. But the final word comes from our editor-in-chief within ten days, and if a writer calls me before that time I won't have any answer. Still, there are those who try to read my body language through the phone, hanging on my every word and pause. It's possible *I* may like something a writer sends in, but it still needs to make the rounds—so be patient.

"Another bugaboo of mine is bad spelling. It gets you off to a really bad start at *TV Guide,* especially if you spell editors' names wrong. Around here, when a manuscript or query makes the rounds, editors circle the misspellings they catch—and there's no doubt in my mind it will adversely affect your chances. Of course, if a piece is strong and compelling, misspellings won't be fatal. But it *will* make us wonder, Can this guy report? How accurate will he be? Your aim is to make a good impression with editors; why set up this psychological roadblock when you can avoid it?

"Frankly, there aren't too many writers who come to us out of the blue with an idea. Many of our stories are written by people in our New York and Los Angeles bureaus; as for the rest, we tend to find them ourselves, usually by reading their stuff in other magazines. When we *do* come across a new freelancer, it's often a one-time deal, where she's writing about something she knows about—like a TV movie that's being shot in her town in Iowa.

"However, there *are* ways to break into the magazine. For instance, I've become the editor of what we call the 'Scoop' section, brief stories that run from half a page to a page in the magazine. Anything can be a 'Scoop' piece—a profile, a piece on technology or the TV industry. One week it was an interview with the star of the *Friday the 13th* series, another it was about TV in Panama under Noriega.

"Since Murdoch took over *TV Guide* in late 1988, our stories have gotten shorter—they're now down to 1,000 to 1,500 words. A piece may run three to four pages in the magazine if it deserves it, but it's rare. Our articles are also more personality oriented than before, but we don't think they're overly sensational. If they did get too sensational, you'd have a lot of unhappy editors here.

"When our new owners came in, we heard they thought the magazine was 'too cerebral.' Yet we've since run a story on [*Sophie's Choice* author] William Styron—and Styron is as cerebral as you can get in a mass-market magazine. The magazine is nothing if not diversified. *TV Guide* offers a real variety; we explore TV from all its angles, and that could include technology, humor, politics, celebrities, service features. Once I drew up a list of categories and came up with about twenty.

"When I think about the writers I like best, the ones that stand out are those who are reliable about meeting deadlines—we have a seven-week lead time on our features. You'd think freelance writers would understand the importance of deadlines; editors certainly take them seriously. Recently we received a piece we'd assigned a year and a half ago! The writer is a newspaper journalist, and he submitted the idea, we okayed it—and then he disappeared for eighteen months. My boss will come to me and say, 'Where's that story?' and I have to be able to give him an answer. It's a writer's job to keep in touch, to let me know if there are problems. Maybe he's doing a profile of a celebrity and the writer is being stonewalled by the publicist. Let us know—maybe we can help move things along.

"I've discovered that there are good reporters and good writers. 'News junkies' tend to be good reporters but only workmanlike writers. Good writers, on the other hand, are wonderful with prose and often not great reporters. We frequently have to rewrite the reporter types and closely fact-check the writer types, but we live with them all; in fact, we *want* both types in the magazine. And as you can imagine, we're thrilled when we find someone with both skills.

"*TV Guide* did well in the last *Writer's Digest* survey [of magazines] for the way we treat writers. We were happy about that—we really care about freelancers."

TV GUIDE, Radnor, PA 19088; (215) 293-8500.
Frequency of Publication: weekly.
Circulation: 16.3 million.

Readership: 56 percent women, 44 percent men; average age thirty-six.
Available Upon Request: free writer's guidelines.
Payment Rate: approximately seventy-five cents a word.

SUSAN SHIPMAN, EDITOR, *VIS À VIS*

"There are a lot of bad writers out there!"

"What do I hate most? Writers who've never seen *Vis à Vis* and presume they can write for us. They're the ones who don't know our stories are around 750 words, and they approach us with totally alien articles that run 3,000 words. I don't understand what leads them to do that! It's like buying a size-14 dress for a size-3 woman.

"People have to know the magazine they want to write for. I realize that *Vis à Vis,* being an in-flight magazine, isn't easy to find, but someone who's serious about writing for us *must* make the effort. We've got a small staff of editors—just five of us—and we run more than thirty short articles each month. Besides the assigning and editing, there's headline and caption writing, fact checking, proofreading, contracts to send out . . . we're so pressed for time. Every call and letter just adds to the volume, and I resent it if the idea is completely inappropriate. Of course, I *don't* resent it if the idea makes sense in terms of who we are and what we do, but otherwise it's very annoying.

"Also, many people who don't know the magazine are under the impression that in-flights use nothing but pickup material. While that may be true of some, it's not true of *Vis à Vis;* all of our material is original. Our pass-along readership totals about 1.5 million each month, and readers are primarily businessmen who obviously do a lot of traveling.

"Interpersonal relationships between editors and writers are so important. You click with some people, and you don't with others. To start with, it's a personality thing: it comes down to how well you get along, if you can sit and talk and joke with the person. As an editor you ask yourself, Is he bringing some smarts to the business? What's his background? Where has he traveled? And finally, do I *like* this person?

"One thing that would definitely *not* make me like someone is a writer who's obviously doing this to get his airfare paid for. The world is changing, and getting free plane tickets just doesn't happen so much; if I get the feeling the person is trying to get an assignment primarily for that reason, it puts me off. We don't send people to destinations simply because they want to go there. However, I *have* found that writers these days seem to get around a lot on their own, and often to the out-of-the-way places we like to feature. So if you've just returned from Auckland or Anchorage and have a good story angle, we may be interested. We split our coverage about equally between domestic and Far Eastern destinations, with an occasional story on Europe. Once United Airlines starts flying in and out of Mexico, we'll be covering that area, too.

"Although I understand that this is a business like any other, I get turned off by writers who seem to be in it just for the money. Some freelancers tend to forget that we're looking for *quality,* not just copy. I don't like someone who submits a second-rate story or tries to push a used, old story idea on me. Too many writers are too relaxed about the work they do. I like to get the feeling that a person *wants* to work and that he cares about his copy.

"While I appreciate a writer who cares about his work, he shouldn't be difficult about it. Cooperation is as important to me as writing ability. I like writers who are cooperative about any rewriting that may be necessary, although I don't expect them to roll over and play dead. Some writers have told me, '*You* fix it!' I feel you should care enough about your article to want to do it yourself.

"Generally speaking, there should be a lot of give-and-take between editor and writer. For example, if a writer has been given an assignment and wants to change the focus of her article because of the research she's done, she should discuss it with her editor, not just go ahead with the change. Similarly, an editor should be open to these kinds of changes—I would criticize any editor who says no to an unreasonable extent.

"I've been asked how much I'm willing to work with a writer. Basically you have to judge how busy you are, and at *Vis à Vis* I'm *so* busy . . . frankly, I don't have time to help a poor writer along. At other magazines, editors may have the luxury of more time and therefore can work closely with a writer who shows potential but may need to hit on a more suitable subject, for example. But the time element here is so pressing that I need people to deliver the goods right off the bat. Apart from the writers I already know and work with, I may make an assignment to an unknown writer who has a good idea and solid clips—with someone like that, I'll often take a chance. However, as I've discovered, there are a lot of bad writers out there!

"I frequently answer my own phone, but I don't like to do it, again for time reasons. I prefer that writers *don't* call— and I certainly don't want to hear from a writer a week after he's submitted an unsolicited query. I may have a foot of mail on my desk after only a week—and that's *nothing* compared to some of the other editors here. Wait a month if you haven't heard from us. And once you get through, please try to be patient with us; keep in mind the frantic pace at which we're working. I try to treat people over the phone with as much courtesy as I can—and hope for the best.

"Honesty—that's very important. I won't work a second

time with anyone who hasn't dealt honestly with me. There's no need for subterfuge in this world."

VIS À VIS (the in-flight magazine of United Airlines), East/West Network, 34 East 51st Street, New York, NY 10022; (212) 888-5900.
Frequency of Publication: monthly.
Circulation: 500,000.
Readership: businesspeople in their late thirties who fly frequently.
Available Upon Request: free writer's guidelines; three dollars for sample copy.
Payment Rate: approximately seventy-five cents a word.

ROSEMARIE LENNON, SENIOR EDITOR, *WOMAN*

"Sometimes we tear our hair out rewriting someone's carelessly written article."

"Without sounding hard-assed, I find that what drives me crazy is lazy work. What I mean by that is, sometimes writers who've worked for me for awhile—who have written terrific stories in the past—start to get sloppy. Many editors have been writers themselves and can tell right away if something is a lazy job.

"What do I mean by a 'lazy job'? That's when a writer has done minimal research and tries to make the article 'fit' the facts she's found, with quotes shoehorned in regardless of whether they're relevant to the original premise. You may have gotten quotes from the requisite three shrinks, but have you answered the questions that were the basis for the article being commissioned? This situation is easy enough to avoid: just reread your letter of assignment before you turn in your manuscript. Have you answered all the editor's questions? Have you covered all the points she wants covered? If not, fix your story.

"I hate when writers think they can get away with doing the minimum. Many times we buy a writer's story and she assumes everything is terrific, but what she *doesn't* know is that the story came *inches* from being killed. And once such a piece is in-house, it may sit in inventory for months or even years because we all dread the task of making it work. Sometimes we tear our hair out rewriting someone's carelessly written article.

"I also resent having to tiptoe around a writer's feelings. It makes me uncomfortable to have to point out faults as well. Yet I recently decided to be honest with one of our contributors. She wrote an article for us that barely made it, and for that reason none of us was very eager to use her again. She's since come back to us with other ideas, all of which were turned down by the editor-in-chief. Finally the writer asked us why, and I admitted her last piece wasn't up to snuff and suggested that perhaps she should come up with smaller, easier story ideas.

"She was so angry! She kept saying, 'I can't believe this! Publishers want me to write *books*!' She finally calmed down when I explained that it would be a waste of everybody's time to jerk her around and that it was better simply to level with her about where she stood at the magazine. Editors don't delight in having to do this sort of thing. Writing is something people get defensive about. I understand—I'm a writer myself. But, frankly, I was horrified by this writer's behavior—I don't like confrontations any more than she does.

"Sometimes writers just astound me by their lack of professionalism. Somebody recently submitted a service article, and it was the worst-written piece—every single sentence was awkward and grammatically off! It looked as though she did nothing more than transcribe her notes and send them in. The editor-in-chief wanted to kill it, but it was a heavily researched piece, and all the information was essentially there; we ultimately felt it was worth it to buy it and fix it in-house. When I called to let the writer know we were using the information but that it nearly got killed and that the article was being turned into a chart, she said, very nonchalantly, 'I knew it had to be edited when I turned it in'!

"Another time I called a writer about her piece, requiring a rewrite. She seemed not at all surprised. She confessed, 'You always ask for a revision, so I just gave you my first draft'!

"I didn't think this point had to be made, but maybe it does: Do your best when you write an article, whether or not it ultimately needs to be revised. Don't simply turn in anything and hope for the best—you may never get another chance to work for that publication.

"And watch your attitude. I hate arrogance in anyone, writer or not. You know . . . the type of person who's *always* angry about something. For example, someone recently approached me, wanting to write for *Woman,* and right off the bat he asked for our top rate of payment, saying he was a professional writer. I didn't doubt he was—his clips proved it—but I insisted that he write his first piece at our starting rate, like everyone else, and quickly assured him that if he was great, he'd get a raise next time. But some writers don't want to prove themselves—and not everyone can write for every publication. This man was one of those writers. He expected me to make an exception in his case and argued his point over and over—and when that happens, I dig in my heels. He finally agreed to take an assignment, but then he called to argue about *expenses,* insisting that he needed to take some of his interview subjects to dinner. *Then* he asked about the rights we were buying and soon he was arguing about *that*. Eventually I started *hating* him. By the time I began preparing his contract I knew I had no interest in working with this person, and I called to say I didn't think it would work and that we should forget it. He said, 'Fine.'

"Look, we're reasonable, and we review situations on a case-by-case basis. We'll raise fees as warranted, and we'll pay expenses within reason, but don't expect everything right away. Until you've proven yourself to us as a valuable contributor, you've pretty much got to play by our rules—but it'll pay off in the end. It's never smart to alienate editors. Even if you know you usually get more money, look at the situation long-term. An editor is *always* desperate for good, reliable writers—you'll more than make up the difference if you prove yourself indispensable to an editor. The best writers, I find, have the best attitudes."

WOMAN, 350 Madison Avenue, New York, NY 10017; (212) 880-8800.
Frequency of Publication: monthly.
Circulation: 600,000.
Readership: women; average age thirty-five.
Available Upon Request: free writer's guidelines with an SASE.
Payment Rate: from five hundred to two thousand dollars.

SALLY KOSLOW, SENIOR EDITOR, *WOMAN'S DAY*

**"Editors want to work with writers who
make *them* look good."**

"I've had mostly good experiences with freelancers. I like working with new writers, and nothing is more gratifying than seeing them develop. I came to *Woman's Day* six years ago, and during that time a number of them have turned into successful, prolific writers. Helping to shape raw talent is something that makes me feel very good.

"One of my favorite *Woman's Day* writers is a joy. I've only met him once—he lives out of town. He's not only prompt, but I would say four times out of five he gets the assignment right on the first go-round. He's simply a delight; I wish I could clone him.

"But I do have some 'problem writers.' My least favorite is a certain individual who always presents his ideas as if you must give them your full attention the moment he phones. Because we request a written proposal for anything we might consider, I have to say, 'Please put your ideas in writing.' Still, he'll call back an hour later and proceed to tell me what the story is about—two calls before noon from a writer I don't really know.

"Calling an editor might be fine if you've developed a relationship and you know she won't mind your phone queries. But don't cry wolf. Don't call again and again. The phone can become my enemy—my time can be eaten up by writers as well as by the tremendous number of publicists who call.

"If I can offer freelancers a tip, it's this: After one successful go-round with an editor at a particular magazine, don't wait for her to tempt you with an idea—try to present another one to her as soon as possible. The writers with whom I've had the most lasting relationships are ones who don't wait for me to bring them an idea, like a cat bringing a bird to its master. Come up with your own good story suggestions.

"Follow-through is so important. Writers who don't deliver, who say they'll write a particular proposal and never do—that bothers me. You've lost the moment. What's more, because I'm counting on your proposal, I will discourage other editors here from assigning a similar story, so we wind up with nothing. Editors want to work with writers who make *them* look good. Meeting the deadline, executing the story, being willing to revise—these are all crucial.

"In general, I respect a writer who *cares* about her work. When I send her a copyedited version of her story before publication, which is our standard procedure, she's concerned enough to evince some interest in it. That expression of caring is so important to me.

"It's wise for writers to establish a stable of noncompetitive magazines. If, for example, one of your ongoing relationships is with a women's service magazine, try branching out to a parenting magazine or one for teenage readers. If I see your byline on a story in a directly competitive publication, I'll wonder if the article idea was your own and, in that case, why you didn't offer it to us first.

"The writer-editor relationship is unique, and I've become friendly with many freelancers whom I like seeing socially. When I'm working on an emotional story, which I enjoy doing, I get to probe and draw out the writer, and if the chemistry is right, I learn a lot about her—sometimes even more than I would about a friend. And because this is a women's magazine, we often do articles on subjects to which I as a wife and mother can personally relate. So I'm usually dealing with writers who can share something that might be helpful in my own life. It's wonderful having things in common with my writers.

"How do you ingratiate yourself to an editor? If you honestly believe that an edit has improved your work, let the editor know. She wouldn't mind hearing that. You might also invite her to lunch or to your home. She doesn't have to say yes if she's too busy, but it shows you think of her as a person. It doesn't *always* have to be business. No editor would be insulted by such an invitation; she'd only be flattered that you thought of her."

WOMAN'S DAY, 1633 Broadway, New York, NY 10019; (212) 767-6000.
Frequency of Publication: seventeen times a year.
Circulation: 4.4 million.
Readership: married women in their thirties with children.
Available Upon Request: free writer's guidelines.
Payment Rate: one dollar a word minimum.

JEANNE MUCHNICK, TRAVEL EDITOR, WOMAN'S WORLD

"I basically don't like writers who try too hard to be my friend."

"With a weird name like *Muchnick,* I've heard my share of taunting nicknames, and as a result I've developed a tough skin when it comes to people mangling my name. But I *still* can't stand it when a freelance writer spells it wrong. It's on the *Woman's World* masthead every week, and it's not such a big deal to look it up. This is one of my major pet peeves in dealing with writers.

"Another is when they have an attitude problem. The other day a freelancer I didn't know called me, saying that she was a world-famous writer who had visited five continents. She asked if I'd done anything on Mississippi and I said that, in fact, we'd recently run a story on Mark Twain's Mississippi. She then asked, 'But was it by a *national* writer?' She sounded surprised when I said yes, but it shut her up. What also happens a lot here is that I get calls from writers announcing that they're off to the Caribbean or to Romania and would I like a story on it—with no focus, no thought to whether or not the destination is appropriate for the *Woman's World* reader.

"Unless you know me and are my friend, *I take no phone queries.* I don't care how experienced you are, how well-published you are, or how many times you've written for *Woman's World;* I want a *written* query with clips—and *no* slides. Because we're a weekly magazine with tight deadlines, I really don't have time to listen to writers drone on about some trip they've taken or plan to take. You'd be surprised how many supposedly experienced writers call me with ideas, even *after* I've told them I don't take phone queries. I'm the kind of person who isn't mean enough to hang up on someone, but I must admit that some writers have made me ruder.

"I also get annoyed by people—especially veteran writers—who don't take the time to look at the magazine. They hear that we use travel stories and then assume that anything goes. But our travel pages usually cover domestic destinations only, with a few Caribbean stories sprinkled in during the year and, once or twice, an 'exotic' location— for example, somewhere in Europe. *Woman's World* readers are very budget conscious, so I can never really feature anything too offbeat or ultradeluxe. However, because many travel writers also write for more upscale books or have recently taken a freebie trip to some exotic isle and are desperate to sell their story, they'll query me about Thailand or Tahiti. *We don't do those kinds of places.*

"Look at *Woman's World*—it's only ninety-five cents a copy. Our stories are short—around four hundred words— and very photo oriented. Stories *must* lend themselves to pictures and include a sidebar on best places to stay, special events, and so on. The stories tend to be themed, such as 'Fort Lauderdale for Families' or 'Stargazing in Los Angeles.' I also like special anniversary stories, such as on Hawaii's thirtieth anniversary of statehood or France's bicentennial. But keep our deadlines in mind—we have a ten-week lead time, although I tend to plan stories as much as six months in advance.

"It may sound callous, but I basically don't like writers who try too hard to be my friend. If we have some common point of reference—say, we've met at a luncheon or you're the friend of a friend—and you call me, get right to the point about what you want. Be yourself. It's fine to want to establish a rapport with me, but don't push it.

"For instance, there's one writer who asks at the beginning of a conversation how I am, although it's quite clear she doesn't care and that she's only interested in making a sale. She then goes into the details of her own life and keeps me on the phone forever. She seems to have no clue whatsoever that I hate her phone calls. Although she's written for *Woman's World* in the past, I have such a personal dislike for her that I don't plan to use her again.

"Don't get the wrong idea—there *are* writers I enjoy working with. Those are the ones who recognize that I'm busy and get right down to business when they call. I also appreciate those who have studied the magazine, submit good ideas, and then follow up after a reasonable amount of time—say, three weeks—because sometimes I get so overloaded I forget to respond.

"I also like writers who are understanding, who realize that occasionally I'm hampered by the politics that exist at the magazine. Often I have to get freelancers' ideas okayed by people above me—I don't always have the final say— and that process can take time. Therefore, I really appreciate writers who are patient, who aren't dying to query someone else so quickly that they can't wait for a response from me. If you're too much in a hurry to give us the time we need to make a decision, take your query somewhere else.

"In addition, I will be very favorably impressed if you've studied the magazine to the point that you know that every travel story features a 'fast fact,' a one- to two-sentence tidbit about the destination in question. If you include a couple of interesting fast facts with your manuscript, I'll be eternally grateful.

"Having said all that, I must also add that I don't buy a lot of freelance travel—I write the vast majority of it myself. However, that's not to say there's no flexibility. If you've got great ideas that are appropriate for *Woman's World,* are easy to work with—and spell my name correctly—you have a good chance of making a sale."

WOMAN'S WORLD, 270 Sylvan Avenue, Englewood Cliffs, NJ 07632; (201) 569-0006.
Frequency of Publication: Weekly.
Circulation: 1.52 million.
Readership: women from twenty-five to fifty-five.
Available Upon Request: free sample copy.
Payment Rate: thirty cents a word.

SUSAN SELIGER, DEPUTY EDITOR,
WORKING MOTHER

"Lyndon Johnson, in describing Gerald Ford, said, 'He can't fart and chew gum at the same time.' I'm looking for a writer who can write and think at the same time—and it's *rare.*"

"Everybody in this business wants to feel she's working with a pro. One of the key indicators that a writer is a pro is that she has a fairly realistic—not an overblown—view of her own talents. A second key is that she displays an awareness of the needs of the magazine she's writing for. There simply is no great story; there *is* a great story for a given magazine. You always have to keep in mind the question, Who is the reader? You should never forget whom you're talking to in your writing. Your attitude at the outset must always be I'm here to give the reader what she needs and wants.

"I don't want somebody to attempt to capture the 'voice' of our magazine—there *is* no single voice in *Working Mother*. You should write in *your* voice. Generally speaking, the best writing is lively, intelligent, conversational. Granted, it's mostly a one-sided conversation! But you as that interesting conversationalist should have lots of good, juicy morsels to share with our reader: solid research, engaging personal stories. Even when a writer is doing a straightforward piece, the right tone of voice is critical. Never talk down; our reader is smart. She also has a job and a family she cares about that keep her incredibly busy. That means you've got to be *lively* in order to capture her attention quickly. Remember, you'll be competing with the kid who's tugging at her skirt and yelling, 'Quit reading that magazine and play with me!'

"The essence of a professional writer is a *cheerful* willingness to stick with the piece until it emerges. The best writer in the world can benefit from a good editor, and I'm happiest when I'm working with a writer who believes that together we're making her piece better.

"Writers often complain that editors don't know what they want or change their minds after they see the finished story, and sometimes it's true. But I believe that often when writers complain about an editor changing her mind, it's *really* a case of the *writer* not delivering. Lyndon Johnson, in describing Gerald Ford, said, 'He can't fart and chew gum at the same time.' I'm looking for a writer who can write and think at the same time—and it's *rare*.

"It behooves you as a writer to follow your editor's directions. Once, one of our senior editors approached a famous writer about doing a piece. The editor's detailed assignment letter gave concrete directions. We never heard from the writer until we received his manuscript with a cover letter. It said, 'Here it is. I tried not to do anything you asked for in your letter. Instead, I came up with a fresh idea.' But his 'fresh idea' was so stale and awful and unreadable that his piece never made it into the magazine.

"If you have an idea or an angle that the editor hasn't considered, talk it over with her before you proceed. By the same token, if during your research you find that there's no *there* there, pick up the phone—don't try to deliver when you know you can't. You might call and say, 'I think the *real* point of the story should be————,' and your editor might tell you, 'Well, we did that two months ago'; or it might be too similar to another piece she recently assigned; or the angle may not be quite right for the readers; or she might say, 'Great idea—go with it!' In general, that check-in call midway through your story, even if everything is fine, can save everybody a lot of anguish.

"An editor I once worked for used to say, 'Things are great when you find the writer and assign the story—until the piece comes in!' And I, a struggling freelance writer, thought, How cruel! *Then* I became an editor! You must remember that we as editors have an emotional investment in your piece, just as you do, and we look forward to the piece working out almost as much as the writer. When a piece comes in and it gleams . . . hell, it makes our day! But the reality is, few pieces come in gleaming, and they usually need considerable polishing. Chances are the editor has a better idea how to fix it than the writer does because the editor has some distance on it. When I make suggestions to a writer and I meet with an enormous amount of resistance—anger, hostility, a prima donna–type don't-touch-a-word-of-my-golden-prose attitude—it's not going to make me want to turn to her again. You've *got* to be able to look soberly at your work. You can object to some changes, of course, but your resistance should be based on the integrity of the piece, not on your ego as a writer.

"On the other hand, it worries me when I hear, 'Change anything!' To me that's a red flag indicating that the writer doesn't care about her piece or her selection of words. It suggests she didn't take that much care in putting the article together. You need the old Aristotelian golden mean.

"When a freelancer doesn't realize that revisions go with the territory, that can be a problem, too. I'm not happy when I hear, 'You said you'd pay me———dollars. Now you want revisions!' The agreed-upon price is for a *printable manuscript.* Writers have to do what needs to be done—within reason, of course—to get the piece in good shape, for their own self-respect, and to placate the editor.

"The process is often slightly painful, I'll admit. While I don't find it painful with most of my writers, there are some rough spots, a tiny bit of prickliness here and there. But if you as the writer try to sustain cheerful enthusiasm, it helps. Life is too short to spend much time working with people who are not pleasant and fun.

"But don't misunderstand—our writers are, for the most part, wonderful, and I feel very lucky. The tone here in the office is calm and cheerful, and the magazine is, too, but not in a namby-pamby way. Most of us—editors *and* freelance writers—are working mothers, just like our readers. Our work and our personal lives are more deeply intertwined than at most other magazines. We're all going through the same thing as our readers—and barely making it through each day alive!'"

WORKING MOTHER, 230 Park Avenue, New York, NY 10169; (212) 551-9412.

122

Frequency of Publication: monthly.

Circulation: 650,000.

Readership: mostly married working women in their late twenties and early thirties with one child and thinking about a second; careers include secretaries, nurses, teachers, and managers.

Available Upon Request: free writer's guidelines and sample copy.

Payment Rate: one dollar a word.

SUCCESSFUL MAGAZINE WRITERS AND WHAT THEY DO RIGHT

JENNIFER ALLEN

Jenny has been a full-time freelance writer for five years. She writes for Architectural Digest, New York, Esquire, New York Woman, 7 Days, Child, *and other magazines, and has contributed to the "Hers" column in* The New York Times.

"A lot of writers get their hearts broken."

"My father was in the magazine business forever—he was an editor at *Reader's Digest*—and that got me started. My first published piece was in *Seventeen,* when I was eighteen. Since then I've written for lots of magazines, and I've worked at a few. I was a guest editor at *Mademoiselle,* on retainer at *New York* magazine, on staff at *Life* . . . I've done book reviews, some profiles for *Esquire.* I'll be starting a new column soon for *7 Days.* The theme will be something along the lines of life in the slow lane. The pieces will be human-interest stories, but more eccentric than your neighborhood school principal.

"Over the years I've found that being a freelance writer is quite an isolated existence. I wrestle with my work all alone, in my little writing room; I don't have a big network. And as a freelancer it's difficult to tell how much power you have over your copy when it comes to editors and being edited; it's hard to learn to stick up for your material. No editor, even the most well meaning, will encourage that in you. But I'm getting better at it. I try not to be obnoxious or lose my temper, but if something is wildly cut or edited without prior discussion, I'll speak up. You should make it clear to your editor that it can't happen again and that you want a say in this.

"A lot of writers get their hearts broken. They send off their copy, and by the end of the editing process their feelings get hurt. I realize it's the editors' magazine. But I always try to read first and second galleys of my stories and let the editors know I want first crack at the necessary cuts. I'm good at cutting—I can usually do it as fast as or faster than the editors. I'm surprised more freelance writers don't insist on doing this. One of my editors once told me, 'You're the only writer we messenger galleys to.' Five years ago I would have said, 'I don't want to be different.' Now I say, 'If that's true, then something's wrong.'

"Writers should insist on seeing galleys of their stories. If they allow an editor to think it's unusual, then it's not the editor's fault if he takes too much into his own hands. It takes courage, especially if you nitpick, as I do. There may be times when I object to a snappier word than the one I used, and I can tell when an editor is breathing heavily on the other end of the phone, anxious to go to lunch, while I'm on the tenth change in the galley. But it's very important for me to do that. Yes, editors are busy, but you have to dig in your heels. You can't worry about their lunch date, even if you like the editor personally. Remember, it's *your* story, and nobody ever says after it's published, 'I bet this piece was better before it was edited.'

"Here's an example. The other day something of mine had been changed—two words—making the copy cutesy. The editor and I had already been through two rewrites; we'd been back and forth on the phone for weeks. So when I called him about these last changes, which would've meant twenty seconds on the phone, I could tell he'd just *had* it. So I let it go—until the next morning. I called, and he was fine about the changes.

"I've also learned that there are times a writer should take her name off her story. It never occurred to me as an option at first, but now I do it all the time. Removing your name won't make page one of the newspaper; it's fairly commonplace and quite self-respecting. It all comes down to the magazine and its editorial practices. For example, some editors freely rewrite writers' copy. That may be *their* experience at magazines, but it's not mine.

"I believe strongly in pride of workmanship. The way you oversee your copy says a lot about your self-image, I think. At the same time I understand that what I'm advocating may be difficult for a full-time freelance writer supporting a family. I'm a wife and mother, but I'm not the sole support of my family. As a writer I make what would pass for a living—in a state other than New York. If, say, I were a single mother, I don't know that I'd be a freelancer. I'd probably get a job.

"If you *have* to turn yourself into a writing factory for

financial reasons, it may be hard to look at your name on the stories you write. Your work then becomes far removed from the reason you started doing it in the first place. You *must* care about what you do! The alternative is becoming a hack. I don't care how many kids you're supporting—it's better to get a job than to have to look in the mirror and say, 'I've written my eight-hundredth hack piece for Magazine X.' Even if you need the dough and have to pay the rent, you can stand up for yourself. To call freelance writing just a business is a rationalization; it's sliding through something that might be difficult for you.

"Whenever I've worried that I'll never hear from an editor again after we've had a protracted situation over one of my stories, he'll often call with an assignment. Editors need you to write for them, particularly since the pay is so bad. They are generally reasonable, and if you present a good case and don't make an ass of yourself, they'll want to continue working with you. Many freelancers believe that if they make themselves heard, the editor will get mad at them, or they'll get squashed. So they end up complaining to their spouse or their friends—never to the editor. But when you *do* voice your objections to the editor, he's usually agreeable. It's really your responsibility to let him know if there's a problem. You think you'll get a reputation for being difficult—but you'll also get a reputation for being good."

DAN CARLINSKY

Dan has been a freelancer for eighteen years and has written for "everything from Seventeen *to* Modern Maturity," *as well as* Playboy, Redbook, Woman's Day, Travel &

Leisure, and Reader's Digest, *among others. He is also the author of two dozen books, including* The Great 1960s Trivia Game *(Harper and Row),* Do You Know Your Husband? *(Price Stern Sloan Inc.) and* Do You Know Your Wife? *(Price Stern Sloan Inc.)*

"If you have half a brain, you don't get into the freelance writing business."

"I started freelancing eighteen years ago, and I often think that if I knew then what I do now, I'm not sure I'd have gone into the business.

"I've spoken two or three times on writers' panels, where neophytes sit at the feet of professional writers to learn from their experiences, and each time I've been the oddball, the naysayer. Repeatedly I've said, 'Go back to your house and find something else to do!' I truly believe that if you have half a brain, you don't get into the freelance writing business. That's because it's populated by people who don't see it as a business. Any housewife or fireman with a word processor is—*zap!*—a freelance writer. So is every unemployed editor, copywriter, or radio producer. *Anyone* can say, 'I'm a freelance writer,' and that applies whether you're good or bad, smart or dumb, trained or untrained. As a result, every editor will tell any writer who pushes too hard, 'I don't need you—there are twenty more writers standing in line behind you.' This is very much a buyer's market and always will be. And so editors, along with often being incompetent and rude, have a patronizing, we-don't-need-you-but-you-need-us attitude toward most writers. Even writers who make six-figure incomes, even those who are sought after, are often treated like dirt.

"Because of this situation, practices go on in this business that would never be accepted in any other. For example, the whole idea of 'kill fees' [a recompense for a commissioned article that is not published] is a scandal. Being offered a kill fee is supposedly a sign that a writer has 'come of age' and no longer has to work on speculation, but it's really a disgraceful way to do business. There's no field I know of where someone can hire you and, if he likes what you do, he'll pay you a set fee, and if he doesn't like what you do, he'll pay only a percentage. It's the same as if I walked into a restaurant, ordered a meal, decided I didn't like it, and offered to pay 25 percent of the check. What you do is you pay and never go back to that restaurant. A magazine should do the same with a professional writer: hire the writer and, if it doesn't like the work, pay in full and never hire that writer again.

"The book business is even crazier than magazines. Most contracts call for you to write your book completely on spec[ulation]. If the publisher doesn't like the manuscript, you're required to give back the advance. Even very experienced authors sign such contracts—and their agents let them, instead of fighting it.

"I would say to someone who still wants to be a freelance writer that even though you're treated like garbage, it's up to you to treat it like a business. You can't be an 'artist' and spend all the time in the world on a piece. I'm not saying be a hack; I'm simply pointing out that you must learn to be efficient. Everyone has a standard of living. Decide what yours is and budget your working time accordingly. For example, if you get an assignment to write a $750 article and it takes you a month to do, and you know you can't live on $750 a month, you have two choices: either write the piece in several days or get more money for it.

"By and large, freelancers are paid at the low end of the white-collar scale. That is, when publishers and editors make up their budget to 'buy words' for their magazines, they're going to pay writers modest rates. I recently read that a freelance stringer for a major national publication was paid $150 a day, which is roughly $37,500 a year. That may sound like a decent wage to a nonprofessional writer, but that doesn't include health insurance, sick time, vacation time, paper clips. . . . So if you earn $37,500 as a freelancer, that may boil down to the equivalent of a $15,000 staff job. You might pay more than that to someone who mows your lawn. There's a reason certain professionals, like models, earn very high per-hour fees—there's no regularity to their schedules and they may not work every day. It should be the same for freelance writers.

"You learn to survive in the business by efficiently marshaling your time, by taking on projects that pay properly on an hourly or daily basis. You always have to be conscious of what you're doing and work with a mental stopwatch. Of course, I occasionally take on something that winds up paying about a dollar an hour because I love it. But you can't do that all the time.

"You also have to learn how to handle the rights you sell to your work and try to resell as much as possible. If, for instance, you write a piece for *Ladies' Home Journal* and then resell it to magazines in Scandinavia and Japan, you become more capitalistic: your past work—your property—is earning money for you while you spend your time doing the next project.

"In my dealings with editors I've discovered that (1) there aren't many left who are that honorable and (2) there aren't many left who are certain of their jobs. At magazines and books, it's hot-and-cold-running editors these days.

"After hearing me say all this, you have good reason to ask why I stay in the business. Obviously I like what I do enough to overlook the problems. But if my best friend asked me about becoming a freelance writer strictly from a business point of view, I'd tell him to forget it."

SHERRY SUIB COHEN

Sherry, a freelancer for fifteen years, writes regularly for Glamour, Bride's, Ladies' Home Journal, Woman's Day, Playgirl, New Woman, Boating, Redbook, Seventeen, *and many other magazines. She is also the author of fourteen books, most recently* Tender Power *(Addison-Wesley).*

"Being a freelancer has enabled me to fulfill all my dreams. I couldn't possibly be happier."

"I started out as a schoolteacher—but then I discovered I could write. Being a freelancer for the past fifteen years has enabled me to fulfill all my dreams. Today I earn a much better living, lead a more exciting life, and meet fascinating people on a regular basis. I couldn't possibly be happier.

"I'd always wanted to write, but I knew I was no Henry James or Jane Austen. The reason I was able to start writing and eventually make a success of it was that I discovered nonfiction. I'm a decent writer and a good researcher, but most of all, I'm a 'people person'—I love people, and it shows. What drew me to the field, apart from the writing itself, was my feeling that the world of writing was a world full of fabulous men and women, particularly editors who, I was convinced, knew secrets I didn't know. I'd always loved reading about editors—stories about Maxwell Perkins delighted me—and I wanted to enter that special world. Becoming a writer has allowed me to do just that.

"I believe one of the reasons I've managed to succeed is that I've deliberately tried to cultivate friendships among my editors. I know it's made them feel better about handing me assignments. Let me give you an example. Before I

131

met Jan Goodwin, the former executive editor at *Ladies' Home Journal*, I'd heard terrible things about her: she was tough, she was scary, she'd bite your head off. Then I had a chance to meet with her in her office. I noticed her English accent, and I made a point of saying I'd just returned from a trip to England. We got to talking, and that personal connection led to a strong, long-lasting friendship—not to mention dozens of well-paying assignments from the *Journal.*

"I believe firmly in the idea of 'nurturing up'—a term I coined in my book *Tender Power.* It's easy to 'nurture down'—massage the ego of those on a level below us. But because we've been taught that it's wrong to cozy up to teachers or others in authority, we're afraid to 'nurture up.' Yet editors, who are in a position to do something for us writers, have egos that need massaging, too. It doesn't matter where the stroking comes from—it's always appreciated if it's sincere.

"How do you develop this ability to win friends and influence editors? You need a sensitivity to others, a sixth sense. If you have a basic interest in people, then you'll be able to find a common ground. It's got to be genuine, though—you can't be a phony baloney.

"The fact is a lot of success in writing comes through personal connections and forming friendships with those who can give you work. It's also a marvelous way to make people love you and to become a part of their lives. You do this not just to get an assignment but to enlarge your circle of friends. What's more, it's totally aboveboard. People working in corporations do this kind of thing on a daily basis. Why shouldn't writers do it with editors?

"If I can do something nice for an editor, I do. I've invited Jan on our boat. I once hosted an engagement shower for one of my editors (but such a personal gesture should be reserved for editors who truly become friends). I give

Christmas presents to every editor I know. And if I don't know an editor that well, I'll send a huge tin of Gummy Bears to the office. I get gifts from some of them, too. I think gift giving is a lovely gesture, and if it turns people off, what can I do? It's a perfectly acceptable business practice and, at the very least, the presents are tax deductible.

"Another thing: I don't believe in abusing the relationships I've formed, and I know I have to do my part. One thing editors hate is writers who miss deadlines, and no one meets a deadline like I do. Even if I have to work all night or all weekend, even if I must sacrifice husband or kids or whatever, I turn in a story on time. And you have to *produce*—you must give editors the best work possible. Being a successful freelancer is more than just giving gifts at holiday time.

"I've also learned that there's nothing to be gained by complaining to an editor, so I never do. I know many writers who lay their problems at the feet of their editors— about how difficult a piece is, how much longer it's taking to finish, how uncooperative the subjects are, and so on. But I feel editors have tough jobs—much tougher than mine. I wouldn't want to be an editor for anything! They don't get as much fame or money as we writers do. They don't get to meet Catherine Deneuve or Estee Lauder or Afghanistani guerillas or take free trips to exotic places. They don't get to go on *Donahue* to promote their books. On any given day I routinely tell myself, 'I can't believe they're *paying* me to do this!' So why bother editors with my meager troubles?

"Similarly, because I'm so grateful to be doing what I'm doing, I do any rewrites that are asked for, instantly and without argument. I don't have as much pride of authorship as some writers do; some of them *hate* when editors tamper with their work. I feel an editor knows what she wants better than I, and I do my best to give it to her.

"Because I have something of a reputation in the magazine field by now, people assume it's a cinch for me to pick up the phone and call anybody I want. The truth is I *despise* the telephone! I sweat and shake before I have to make certain business calls. So I write a lot of postcards or notes instead; it's easier for me.

"The most valuable aspect of my becoming a writer has been the wonderful friendships I've made over the years—and I've learned, to my delight, that it isn't difficult to make friends in this profession. Even if I never wrote another word, I'd still be glad I met and became close with so many terrific people."

MARY ALICE KELLOGG

Mary Alice, formerly senior editor at Parade, *a correspondent and associate editor of* Newsweek, *and a columnist for* Glamour, TV Guide, *and* Seventeen, *has been freelancing full-time for the last ten years. She is a frequent contributor to* Bride's, Vis à Vis, GQ, Travel & Leisure, Harper's Bazaar, *and* Cosmopolitan, *and is the author of* The Last Best Place to Be *(Doubleday) and* The Life-Planner *(Simon & Schuster).*

"It's difficult once you . . . find yourself working with self-indulgent little weenies who haven't edited a day in their lives."

"Many would-be freelance writers think, If I fail as a brain surgeon (or secretary or whatever), I can always freelance. But that's not true. It takes a very specific type of person with a very specific attitude to be a successful free-lancer.

"At the beginning I had a great magazine-writing reputation, and for a long time I thought the world would come to me. It didn't. I had never developed a 'marketing head'; I didn't think about how my writing could fill specific magazines' needs. I was too scattershot and sent articles everywhere instead of concentrating on a few markets and getting to know a handful of editors. Over time I became more businesslike—I *had* to.

"For example, right after I'd gotten my advance to write *The Last Best Place to Be,* I went to Arizona, primarily to do research for the book. While I was there, I also did a roundup on the best restaurants in Phoenix for one of the in-flight magazines, and I wrote a profile of a local celebrity for another magazine. Before each subsequent trip I'd call editors I knew and say, 'I'm going to Arizona. Here are some wonderful ideas. . . ,' and I'd get assignments. This way I was able to work on articles and the book at the same time, which was great, especially since most of my book advance had been swallowed up, thanks to the new tax law.

"Over the years I discovered that one hazard of freelance writing is burnout. Lately my schedule has been to work on a chapter of my book for a week, then do all my magazine stuff—sometimes as many as three stories in a week. At the same time I have to follow up with editors: send out new queries to keep the cash flow going, goose the accounting departments about my checks, do interviews and research for current assignments. Then I go back to some concentrated work on my book. I'd love to get just one book to do and not hustle so much. In fact, there was a period a few years ago when I felt, *This is getting crazy!* I was working constantly, including a lot of travel, but I found it counterproductive.

"Now I take off weekends and legal holidays, and work

135

like a dog the rest of the time. I find I need to be recharged every now and then, and I do that by taking time off. I can tell from my writing how tired I am; when I'm exhausted, I may take an extra-long weekend during which I won't make lists or go into my home office at all. Being a free-lancer means looking at everything in your life, including your cat, as a potential story. If I see that happening too much, it's another sign that I need to take a breather. That habit is hard to turn off—it's a part of you, especially if you're a generalist, as I am.

"Another pitfall of freelancing is having to deal with edi-tors who aren't as professional as I am. It's difficult once you've reached a top professional level and find yourself working with self-indulgent little weenies who haven't ed-ited a day in their lives.

"Not long ago I got a new editor at one magazine where I'd been doing a column, and he knew nothing about the subject. He asked me to write about a TV show that had been canceled a year and a half earlier! Another editor at a travel magazine I work for wanted me to give him an esti-mated budget for a trip I had scheduled to San Francisco. He asked how much I was planning on *eating* and whether I could get a hotel for under fifty dollars a night. I thought, Has he crawled out from under a rock? I told him it was absurd—this was a major national magazine with a hefty budget. Yet another editor added quotes to a story of mine *after* he'd sent me final galleys to read. The piece came out and I was furious! This was *not* my beautiful story! Luckily it wasn't libelous. When you find yourself in situations like these, remember: You can always vote with your feet. You never have to work again with an editor who is incompe-tent or unethical. It's just not worth it.

"Another thing I hate is when an editor isn't focused enough and *I* end up doing remedial counseling. For in-stance, someone will call and say, 'I want a piece on love . . .' and I have to force the editor to focus on what she really wants, for *my* protection. So I end up doing not only my job, but the editor's as well. That abdication of responsibility on an editor's part is unprofessional, and if I even *sniff* it anywhere, I won't work with that editor.

"You must also learn when to cut your losses with a magazine. One women's magazine asked me for some ideas for essays, and eventually they gave me an assignment. I wrote the piece, and my editor called to say, 'There's a problem with your essay—it's in the first person. Oh, and there's another problem—it has a point of view.' I didn't know what planet she was on! When an editor starts talking like this, it's a no-win situation. My time is valuable and, anyway, I knew I could sell the piece elsewhere. All I said to her was, 'Make sure my kill fee is in the mail,' and I sent the piece to another magazine, which accepted it right away.

"It's also smart to nudge editors who hold onto your stories forever. I've had pieces that were held in inventory for three years. Now if a magazine has had one of my stories for a year, I'll call and say, 'Look, you've had it for a year. Is it likely to run?' If they say no, I take it elsewhere. If they say, 'We don't know,' then I urge them to schedule it as soon as possible. As a former editor, I understand how these things happen: editors will assign a story and buy it, but it's not high on their list, or they may get bored with the subject and it may sit in inventory forever. But as a writer, you need to *force* them to be straight with you about the fate of your work. If editors aren't straight with me—and the woods are filled with them—I won't work with them. It's important to get paid, but it's also important to get *published.*

"Some editors are like little sheep, huddled together. It may take another editor at another magazine to have the courage to run your piece. If you have good instincts, trust them. Say, 'I'm not chopped liver here! I have —————— years experience as a writer. I'm a professional!' It's like any other relationship: if you let people treat you like a door-mat, they will."

VANDA KREFFT

Vanda has been a full-time freelancer for ten years. She's a frequent contributor to Elle, New Woman, Woman's World, The Star, *and other magazines.*

"When an editor doesn't have a face or a shape, we tend to deify him—but editors aren't gods."

"One thing I've learned in my years as a freelance writer is the customer is always right. No matter how you slave over a story, even if it's a work of art to you, it's still a *product* and the editor is buying this product. Since he's agreeing to give you money for it, he's entitled to get what he wants. Even if his vision of the piece is different from yours, you've got to give him what he wants. Put your pride aside, *listen* to his criticism—and make whatever changes he feels are necessary. I always try to listen to what *his* concept of who his reader is and apply his comments to what I've done. And no matter what you've written, it can always be improved. You can always end up with some-thing better if you cooperate and follow his suggestions.

"In keeping with the notion that the customer is always right, I believe it's okay to let an editor yell at you from time to time—even when it's clear it's not your fault. Edi-tors are in high-pressure situations—they may be pushed in all directions and may disagree with their boss's demands. Editors are expected to be good soldiers, and sometimes they yell at writers just to let off steam.

"I remember an editor I'd worked with for several years—I'd always done my best for him. He knew from experience I was totally trustworthy. Then one day he called to say his boss was questioning a quote in my story that I'd gotten from a psychiatrist. The editors actually believed I'd made up the quote, which of course I hadn't—I had the interview on tape. Eventually they were convinced my quote was accurate. But instead of saying, 'How dare you!' I just figured my editor had had a bad day, and I let it pass. That was a smart move: the next day he asked his secretary to call me back to apologize. I knew the evidence proved my honesty more persuasively than I could have by angrily defending myself, and I didn't want to make the editor feel worse about all this.

"In general, it's more important to decide if this is a person you want to work for in the future than to be right at this moment. Should you exacerbate the situation or let it slide, knowing you want to continue a relationship with this editor? It's your job as a writer to 'take it' sometimes; you can know. you're right without always having to prove it.

"Because I do a lot of celebrity profiles, I come into regular phone contact with publicists, as well as secretaries and assistants. You have to be smart about how to deal with these go-betweens—it can greatly affect your success as a freelancer. Remember, these people control access to the person you want; if you dismiss them as nothing more than receptionists or mail openers, you can hurt your chances to see your interview subjects. If you're rude or condescending to a publicist, for example, she may misrepresent you to the celebrity, and if you aren't nice to an editor's assistant, she may 'lose' your payment for weeks or months.

"Conversely, if these people—especially a star's publicist—like you, they can give you an entree to the celebrity you might not get on the strength of your credentials alone. If there's a limit to how much publicity a star will do (and there usually is), a publicist who likes you because you've been friendly may encourage the celeb to talk to you in preference to some other writers.

"How do you boost your status with a magazine editor? Be the one to go the extra mile that nobody else will go. Believe me, it'll pay off later. If you're the person who can be counted on for the fast, thorough rewrite or that extra celebrity quote even though the star's publicist has bitten your head off, you'll earn points with any decent editor. Maybe next time he'll toss you an easy assignment.

"I'll give you an example. I once did a cover story on Anjelica Huston for a magazine, and it was probably the hardest piece I ever had to write from the standpoint of time constraints. The piece had to be turned in to the magazine in order to coincide with the announcement of the Academy Award winners—she won the Best Actress Oscar that year—and it meant interviewing Anjelica on a Friday and Federal Expressing the two-thousand-word story on Monday morning. I had to transcribe a three-hour tape, and to make it even more difficult, there had been very little published about her at the time, so I didn't have much in the way of background. But I took the assignment knowing it would be a killer, and the editors loved the story. What's more, my stock at that magazine shot up, and I got a couple of assignments later on that were the editors' ideas.

"Another tip: don't hold grudges against magazines. Once an editor at a women's magazine gave me an assignment that involved traveling to a movie set in London and conducting several interviews, all of which I did. But when I got back, I learned that another editor had come in, taken over the idea—and reassigned it to another writer! I screamed and yelled to my friends about what had happened, but not to the editors in question. If you make yourself a complainer, editors don't hear if you're right or wrong—only that you're a complainer.

"The same is true if a story of yours gets killed, even if it's for a reason you disagree with. The main thing is to get your kill fee, move on, and try to get another assignment from the magazine. Of course, this is hard to do when you feel like screaming, but there's no point—you'll only harm your relationship with the editor.

"But I don't believe you should be a wimp, either. When you find yourself dealing with a particularly difficult editor, you have to come to the point where you recognize, *This isn't going to work.* This person has different standards and opinions from yours, and when you start to feel that dealing with him is like constantly hitting your head against the wall, you have to cut loose and move on. Otherwise, you risk diminishing your self-confidence. You need to work with people who are on your wavelength, not people who are trying to turn you into a totally different animal. This is especially true for us writers who frequently work with editors we've never met in person. When an editor doesn't have a face or a shape, we tend to deify him—but editors aren't gods. They can be unprofessional, and they can be wrong. And at that point you must take responsibility for yourself and your own career, and realize that these people won't help you get to where you want to go."

WILLIAM MARSANO

Bill has been freelancing full-time for five years and contributes regularly to such magazines as Condé Nast Traveler, GQ, Connoisseur, TV Guide, *and* Ladies' Home Journal. *He specializes in travel, but also writes on new products, electronics, and celebrities.*

"Some editors are unscrupulous and must be approached with caution."

"It's vital that a writer become known by editors, but how do you do that without a recommendation from another writer? It's like saying, 'Come back when you have experience.' The best way to get an editor's attention is to show solid writing credits and send a pitch letter that will draw a positive response.

"Unfortunately, these days you'll find more and more editors won't take the time to respond to a written query unless it's terrific. So a writer must find a way to write an efficient pitch—efficient in terms of not devouring an enormous amount of his time and in terms of getting an editor to give him an assignment. Don't forget, people who call themselves writers are a dime a dozen, so the more convincing your pitch, the less you'll seem like the rest of the dozen.

"After an initial assignment, the best way to develop your relationship with an editor is by giving him help when he needs it. If an editor *ever* calls you and needs you to write something, there's no question: you do not say no, whatever else is going on in your life. You work seven days that week if you have to, and you give him a good article— on time. You make that piece as good as if you had a month to do it. You can't have the attitude that just because it's the editor's emergency it shouldn't be *yours,* too. It must be a terrific piece, not just 'pretty good, considering . . .' Help out an editor this way and he'll remember you.

"I've found that one of the biggest problems in dealing

with magazine editors is that an assignment will be given on a flimsy basis. That is, an editor may call me with a general idea for a piece, and he'll say, 'See what you can do with this . . .' The idea is not fully formed in his mind—sometimes he won't really know what he wants until he's seen the manuscript. It's all too easy for a writer and an editor to miscommunicate on a story, and when that happens, you'll have trouble—and a lot of extra work ahead of you.

"The same thing might also happen because at many magazines the manuscripts are commented on by *several* editors, and an editor other than yours may ask for something entirely different. Again, this translates into more work for you. The freelancer often becomes a victim. In the end, all these changes may ultimately produce a better story, but editors need to formulate the story idea in the first place. If you sense the idea is too diffuse or vague, you must nail your editor down as much as possible.

"Some editors are unscrupulous and must be approached with caution. Remember, they will have some say over the payment you receive for your story, and they may ask you to accept too low a rate with the promise that things will improve. If they don't very soon, chances are they won't in the long run. At the beginning of your career, when you need to gather credits, it'll be difficult to turn down *any* assignments. But now and then you'll have to refuse those editors who take advantage of you. A magazine editor gets his paycheck every Friday; you get yours when you can. He won't see your fiscal needs in the same way you do. You must work with someone who helps you get paid better, who'll assure you of more expense money, and so on. Get out early on if you see your editor isn't legitimately representing you.

"Why is this so important? If you don't get out, you'll start doing sloppy work, because you'll feel that's all it's worth, and that will damage your reputation. You can't take a clip of a mediocre story you wrote to the next editor and say, 'I would've done a better job if the magazine had paid better.' Always do the best work you're capable of doing. Some writers think they need only submit a draft and their editor will polish it. That's very unprofessional. Editors don't work for *you;* you work for the editor. And if the editor is lazy or not as good as *he* should be, he may place too much faith in your piece as it's turned in and not catch all your mistakes.

"This applies not only to the writing but to the accuracy of your story. Just as your manuscript should ideally go through the editor with a minimal amount of rearranging, it should also go through the fact-checking department with ease. Writers who introduce errors into their text out of carelessness or laziness hurt themselves. We all make typos in recording a price or a phone number here and there. But if you've made a serious mistake because you haven't bothered to look something up, editors won't trust you—and won't work with you.

"Another good thing for freelancers to do is to know other writers and communicate with them regularly. Writing is a lonely profession, but what makes it lonely isn't sitting in front of the word-processor screen but *looking for work.* You need friends in the business you can occasionally chew the rag with. It's helpful for a number of reasons: You learn which editors to be wary of. You find out which magazines are looking for what. And you exchange tips in general. Never hold back tips—you've got to help out the next guy. You'll see that that sort of thing will enable *you* to progress faster, and they'll help you when you need some information or someone to talk to. When I first came back to New York after having been away for fifteen years, I didn't know many writers, and it was pretty grim.

"If you're a writer with line-editing skills, it's smart to take on some freelance editing work if you can. It's a good way not only to meet editors but also to learn how magazines work, to find out what's wanted in terms of stories and what isn't. In addition, freelance editing helps your writing by sharpening your eye and ear. And it's a way to earn some cash between assignments."

SARA NELSON

Sara has been freelancing full-time since 1984; previously she worked as an editor at Redbook *and as a staff writer at* Self. *She writes for those two magazines as well as for* Mirabella, 7 Days, Glamour, Connoisseur, New York Woman, The Wall Street Journal, *and* Seventeen.

"Learn to become a master of the short phone call."

"Over the years I've learned something that's proven very valuable to me as a freelancer: not to talk too much about my proposal during the assigning stage.

"During lunch with an editor I'd routinely discuss my best stuff, all the juiciest anecdotes and examples I planned to use in my next story for her. But then once I submitted the piece, I'd often hear a disappointed 'It had a lot of what you already told me.' In other words, editors want to believe you did more work on the story than simply what you told them off the top of your head over lunch. So be judicious in what you tell the editor about your assignment. You've got to let her know *something* of what to expect, but not everything.

"That piece of advice can also work the opposite way.

What I mean is, sometimes I'll discuss certain things I *think* I'll be including in the story, and then not be able to include them. For example, I may say that I plan to interview not only a particular celebrity but also his wife. Then I get to the interview and find out the celebrity refuses to let his wife talk to me. So I write the story as best I can without the wife's comments, and then I may hear from my editor, 'Where are the quotes from the wife?' Sometimes you can't help it—you can't always get the material you want to get, or when you write the story, you realize some stuff just doesn't work, so you deliberately leave it out. If you haven't discussed it in too much detail ahead of time, you will avoid trouble. I've learned to say a little less about any story I'm working on. If I have four things to tell an editor, I may only say two—the two that I'm most sure will make the cut. Aim for an article that includes the things she expects *plus* something new.

"Editors tend to have a wish list—twenty or so questions they'd love to have answered in the piece, or so they think at the beginning. But as you get involved in researching the story and become the expert, you'll discover that some of what the editor has asked for is outside the scope of the piece you're writing. Remember, editors don't necessarily have a tight focus on the story to begin with—you have to go with your own instincts about it. Still, whenever that used to happen to me, I'd panic. I'd say to myself, 'Oh my God . . . I didn't include anything about the way the apartment is decorated!' Now I may choose to omit some of what the editor has mentioned because I've decided it just doesn't fit—and I know that once he sees what I've written, he'll realize many of his original questions are not screaming to be answered.

"For example, I do a lot of celebrity pieces, but I also do stories about people in the news who are not so high-profile. There may not be a lot already published about someone you're assigned to do, and nobody is really sure what this person is like. After the interview(s), then, it's up to you to go back to your editor and correct any misconceptions he may have. You have to say, 'Look, I've talked to her and these are my perceptions.' After a while your editor will trust you.

"So the moral is: listen to everything your editor says he wants, but recognize that once you've done the work, *you* have a more complete picture than he does, and it's up to you to pick and choose the relevant points.

"I've changed a bit in the way I use the phone. Once I would call my editor every step of the way. I do that much less now. So much of it has to do with the nature of the piece and your relationship with the editor. I've found from talking to my writer friends that it's okay to feel insecure about an assignment, no matter how established you are, and calling an editor to discuss your story may be a big help. But you have to really know the person and how much he may or may not mind your calls. If I don't know an editor very well, I won't bug him unless there's a major change in the piece.

"One editor who's become a close friend, Judy Coyne of *Glamour,* says it's important for every freelancer to learn to become a master of the short phone call, and she's right. Basically it's, Hi, how are you, here's my question, get the answer, thank you, and good-bye. I'm trying to move more in that direction.

"I also try to be smart about *when* I call. For example, I know that *7 Days* is a weekly and that its feature pages close on Monday evening. So if I were to call an editor about next week's piece on Monday night when he's closing *this* week's issue, he'd be understandably annoyed. Sometimes, if I have a question for an editor and it's not urgent, I will call her at lunchtime when I know she's not there, and I'll leave a message. This way she can call when it's convenient for her. And I try to be specific when I leave a message. I'll say something like, 'I have a quick question about the incest story; please call back when you can.' A good editor will call you back promptly, and at the same time, you leave her with the feeling that *she's* in control.

"I've also learned not to do much bragging (or complaining) to editors. For example, I used to talk to my editors a lot about how long stories were taking me to write, as a way to show how hard I was working. Now, of course, I'm more experienced and things don't take me as long. But the point is editors don't *really* want to know how long a piece took or what you had to go through—they simply want the piece, and they want it to be good. They know that just because something took you a long time it's no guarantee it's good—just as you know that because something went quickly for you doesn't mean it's lousy. Sometimes a 1,000-word essay can take three times as long as a 2,500-word researched piece—things that come straight out of your head can be more difficult. The editor's feeling about it may be, 'We talked about it, it's only an essay—what's the big deal?' But it *is* a big deal to you."

ANTONIA VAN DER MEER

Tony has been a full-time freelancer for six years, contributing to dozens of magazines, including Cosmopolitan, Redbook, Mademoiselle, Bride's, Child, Good Housekeeping, Weight Watchers Magazine, *and many others. She has published five books, including* Parenting Your Premature Baby *(Henry Holt) and* The Private Adoption Handbook *(Villard).*

"As a freelancer you hold every position in your company—you're the secretary, treasurer, bookkeeper, and manufacturer of the widget."

"If I'm successful, it's because I'm extremely persistent as a freelancer. A lot of writers send out one or two queries and once they get a rejection, they give up. Writers have to believe in their ideas and keep trying—there's no time to rest! If you don't keep knocking on editors' doors, they'll quickly forget you. Even after all the articles and books I've published, editors seldom call me; *I* have to look for *them*. If you wait around for an editor to phone you, you'll be waiting a long time. They have lots of writers at their disposal, and it's rare that they're searching for new ones.

"And *getting* ideas isn't enough; it's where you *place* them. You may have a good idea that could still be rejected by ten magazines because it's not appropriate for them. You must study magazines you intend to write for to see what they're doing *now* and whether your ideas are suitable.

"Developing a good relationship with an editor often means sharing a piece of personal information that may work to your advantage. For example, if you're a newlywed, mention that in your query to *Bride's*. Planning on writing for *Child*? Let them know you have a preschooler.

"When you start out as a freelancer you'll be anxious to take every assignment you can get, and you should—you'll have steady work and get good experience. But there will come a time in your career when saying yes to everything can be counterproductive. After a number of years it's good to determine what's worth your time and what you enjoy writing about. Turning down work when an editor approaches you isn't easy, but sometimes you have to.

"I'm always astounded by young writers who tell me they've taken on an assignment without knowing how much they'll be earning. Freelance writing is a *business,* and you shouldn't forget that in the excitement of getting an assignment.

"Another thing that surprises me: when writers aren't aware of the rights they're selling. I was lucky—I was an editor at *Seventeen* magazine before I started freelancing, and I knew what a contract was and the different kinds of rights we bought from writers. Some freelancers don't realize, for example, that their checks may be stamped with a statement indicating they're signing away all rights to their story. You have to be assertive enough to call your editor when that happens and insist on only selling first North American rights. Better yet, find out the magazine's rights policy *before* you accept an assignment. And be wary of 'work for hire' contracts—most professional freelancers refuse to write for publications that use such agreements.

"These days I've learned to be more assertive in general. I've come to realize over the years that what I'm selling to an editor is a good product, and I've learned how to ask for more money and to fight to retain as many rights to my articles as I can. I'm more willing than ever before to ask an editor for what I want. I only wish I had done it sooner.

"In fact, now that I've been doing this, it's rare when I ask for more money and *not* get it. I may request an additional three hundred dollars and only get one hundred dollars, but it's one hundred dollars more than if I hadn't said anything. I also turn down work now when editors won't give me what I consider to be a fair price for an assignment, so they know I'm serious.

"I'm serious about my work habits, too. If, for instance, a query gets rejected, I force myself to send it out again to a different magazine within a week—I don't give myself time to get depressed. I simply tell myself I sent the idea to the wrong magazine the first time. I've sold plenty of pieces to good magazines after they've been turned down elsewhere. It just reinforces my theory that you have to keep going until you find the right home for every article and idea.

"Keep an idea file, as I do. Whenever I get a promising idea for an article but am too busy to flesh it out into a good query, I jot it down. Then, about once a month I go through the ones I've collected and send out as many queries as possible to as many different magazines as I can. Little by little the assignments trickle in. I find this system a good way to avoid dry spells.

"I manage my writing like a *business*. I have an office at home, and I go into it every day and really *sit* there and write from nine to five or ten to six. It also feels like a real job to me because of the financial system I set up when I first got started. For a long time I would put all the checks I received into an interest-bearing savings account. Then, every two weeks I would withdraw a fixed amount and deposit that into a checking account. In effect, I was putting myself 'on salary.' I found it very helpful because I then avoided the temptation to, say, blow a two-thousand-dollar check on a new wardrobe. It also gave me a 'steady income,' another way of helping me see my freelancing as a serious business.

"Remember, as a freelancer you hold every position in your company—you're the secretary, treasurer, bookkeeper, and manufacturer of the widget. And you have to be as good at being the treasurer and getting the money as you are at your writing if you want to be successful."

IRA WOLFMAN

Ira has been a magazine writer and editor for ten years and a full-time freelancer for five. He contributes regularly to Travel & Leisure, Spy, Architectural Record, Diversion, Family Circle, Child, *and many other magazines, as well as writes an architecture column,* "Skyline," *in the* New York *Sunday Daily News Magazine. He's the author of* The Official Ellis Island Book of Genealogy *(Workman).*

"I went completely crazy. I threw things around my apartment. . . . I thought, How *dare* they treat a professional this way!"

"I have a few basic dos and don'ts for beginning freelancers. First, never write 'First North American rights' at the top of your manuscript. It says that you've just read the Junior Writer's Manual, and any editor who sees that will laugh and think, 'This person isn't a professional.' Another big don't: Don't send twelve ideas to an editor at one time. It indicates that you haven't thought out your ideas, that you haven't really studied the magazine. Never send more than two or three carefully selected suggestions appropriate to the magazine you want to write for.

"If you're just starting out, start small—as in, small article. You can break into even the best, most prestigious magazines if you try to come up with a suitable idea for one of their front-of-the-book sections, like *New York* magazine's 'Fast Track' or *Connoisseur's* 'Connoisseur's World.' What's nice about aiming for these columns is that you get your foot in the door, you get good clips—and you can still rightly say you've been published in a major magazine, even if your story is only five hundred words long.

"One of the biggest mistakes new writers make is taking rejections personally. I'll never forget one horrible episode with a travel editor of a major daily newspaper. I'd just gotten back from a trip to Belgium, where I'd discovered some fabulous architecture, a subject I specialize in. I called this editor—someone I knew—and proposed a story on a walking tour of Art Nouveau buildings in Brussels. He suggested I do some checking to make sure a similar story hadn't run in his publication within the last few years and then pitch the idea to his boss. I checked—no such story—and then I wrote the query. I even included a small map of the places I planned to cover. Around ten days later, after all that time and work I'd put in, I got back a three-by-five-inch form rejection slip saying, 'Thank you for thnking [*sic*] of us.'

"Well, I went completely crazy. I threw things around my apartment and wasted many valuable hours bitching to my friends about what had happened. I am a professional, I thought. How *dare* they treat a professional this way! But they did—and after a while I calmed down and went on to the next thing. I realize now that had I followed up with other well-thought-out ideas for that travel section, eventually I would've gotten an assignment—I would have had some extra leverage by playing on the editors' guilt. That technique has worked at magazines I've subsequently written for. The moral of the story? Don't take magazine rejections too much to heart. Have a lot of projects going at once so that no single disappointment will devastate you.

"I also strongly suggest you be nice to magazine employees who aren't very high up on the totem pole—it'll pay off in the end. At one magazine I tried to break into, I found myself dealing with a junior editor—his title was 'senior editor' but there were about fifteen names above his on the

masthead. Anyway, I kept sending him three or four queries, and even though he rejected them, he was very professional and supportive. After the last rejection I sent him a
note to tell him I appreciated his sensitivity and help-
fulness. Boy, did he appreciate that! He called to say he'd
never gotten a letter like mine before, and I know it moti-
vated him to help me that much more. Soon after, I got an
assignment from his magazine.

"I don't consider this manipulative in the worst sense.
Junior editors often have more time and interest in cultivat-
ing unknown-yet-talented writers—after all, bringing in a
good, new writer is a feather in their cap. Writing a brief
note of appreciation or being friendly to an editor's secretary and not just treating her like a serf is an easy thing to
do and can really pay off.

"Telephone etiquette is also very important. Whenever I
call an editor I always say, 'Is this a convenient time to
talk?' and if it isn't, I ask when I should call back. It gives
her an 'out' if she needs one, and it also shows your sensitivity, that she can count on you not to annoy her. And if
you want to make direct contact with an editor, try calling
before 9:00 A.M. or after 5:00 P.M., when his assistant isn't
likely to be around.

"Once you get an assignment, don't be afraid to help
your editor shape and narrow it if it seems unclear to you.
Many writers, especially beginners, assume editors always
know exactly what they want. They don't. I was recently
given an assignment from a major women's magazine to do
a piece on discrimination against women and the law—*all*
facets of the law. Stupidly I said, 'Okay, I'll do it.' It wasn't
until I started doing my voluminous research that I discovered just how massive this topic was and that it could
never be adequately covered in the three thousand words
they asked for.

"So as soon as you suspect that the topic you've been

assigned is simply too unwieldy or too unfocused, say so—
otherwise you'll be doing a lot of work on an article that
will probably never get published. If the editor insists she
can't get more specific about what she wants, force her to
take a stab at it—and get it down in writing in her letter of
assignment.

"One last thought: Writers alone can't have a lot of impact. But I'm a member of the New York–based National
Writers Union, and I've found them very helpful as a support group and with grievances against publications, such as
collecting money from late-paying magazines, or ones that
have folded. I advise you to contact them."

DAN YAKIR

*Dan has been a full-time freelance writer spe-
cializing in film for eleven years. His publishing credits include* Elle, US, European Travel
and Life, Film Comment, New York, American Film, Rolling Stone, *and* Interview.

**"Freelance magazine writing is like going to
war. You have a mission—to get published—
and don't bother to come back unless you're
victorious!"**

"I've been fairly successful as a freelancer, and yet the
more I look at it, the more I realize how arbitrary and ten-
uous the editor-writer relationship is. At the base of that
relationship, of course, is what the editor thinks of your
writing. But beyond that, it comes down to: Can he or she
imagine dealing with you for any period of time?

"Whenever I'm about to meet a new editor, I have a

system I use. I go to that person's office and present my case. We usually exchange opinions about movies, about people, about the movie-making industry. This gives the editor the chance to see if there's a 'common language' between us. I've never had a situation with a new editor where I felt, This isn't going to work out. I always believe in a common denominator. The two of you may disagree philosophically, but you can always try to find a common ground. At such a meeting, the writer hopes the relationship will work out and prove lasting; the editor is usually optimistic, too, and curious at the very least.

"Of course, there are exceptions. A magazine editor and I had a mutual friend, and the editor invited me for coffee, to discuss ideas. I came prepared with a list of appropriate ideas and she liked them wholeheartedly. She also seemed to like me as a person—we wound up spending the day together shopping. She told me she'd talk over my ideas with her colleagues and get back to me.

"The following week, when I hadn't heard from her, I called to get her response. For whatever reason, I was never able to get her on the phone. To this day—and that was about five years ago—I still haven't heard from her and still don't know why. I could've handled a no from her; I'm a professional and have been dealing with editors for years. But she simply proved unreliable. That's why I say you can't plan the way a relationship with an editor will turn out—it's so fragile and intangible. Anything could happen to change it—a bad mood, a tough day at the office, anything.

"I've learned over the years that personality is very important to the writer-editor relationship. I'd like to think that the writing is all, but that's simply not the case. If an editor takes a dislike to you, you could be a Pulitzer Prize winner and it wouldn't matter. I've never tried to get work by shmoozing at parties, even though I know it's done all the time. I've discovered that an editor who loves you at a party may be in a terrible mood at the office the next day and may not want to work with you.

"To give you an example of the fragile nature of this business, I'll tell you what happened to me at one magazine. I had been listed on the masthead as a contributing editor—I'd done many cover stories for them that were well-received by the staff and throughout the industry. Then a new editor-in-chief came in, and the first thing she did was remove from the masthead the names of some contributing editors before even meeting them, including me. I asked her for a meeting. It took about a month's worth of calls to her office and some pressure from allies I had on the staff before she agreed to see me. When she did, she told me, 'Write for us again and we'll put you back on the masthead.' Although she said my ideas were good, nothing ever materialized. She brought in new people, mostly her friends.

"This happens all the time, in *every* business, so you as an individual freelancer have to be prepared—by having *many* outlets for your work. If you only have one or two and they go down the drain, you'll be in trouble. So have a thousand. I know what my major outlets are at any given time, and I realize that a year from now they could be totally different. I'm prepared.

"Another tip: Be reliable and available. My tendency is to offer an editor ideas that interest me, but that's only *half* the story. You always have to be available to an editor who has desires of his own. My policy is to try never to say no to editors. I believe that if you're reliable, they'll turn to you when they need someone.

"When it comes to deadlines, I always meet 'real' deadlines—experience will tell you if a deadline is real or not. When you call to see if an editor has read your piece, that's when you'll know. I've often killed myself to meet a so-called deadline, only to phone two weeks later to find the editor still hasn't looked at my story. Editors lie shamelessly about when they need a piece. When I first started out, I'd always turn in the piece when it was asked for—some editors have a neurotic fear that a writer will die in midassignment. He or she may want the piece as much as a month early, but that can compromise the quality of the work. If a deadline is legitimate, though, I'll do everything in my power to meet it. And if I find I need more time, I'll call—that's learned wisdom. I try to make sure I have enough time to do a good job without going crazy about it.

"It sounds trite, but do the best work you can. You have to believe you've done your best, and hopefully it's unique or so personal that no one else could do it just that way. Develop a style, an approach to your writing that distinguishes you—the fantasy a writer has is that his story is so identifiable that people can pick out his article even without his byline on it.

"You've heard it time and time again, but it's still true: Don't take rejection or criticism of your work personally. Even after I'd been widely published I encountered editors who were very condescending, who seemed to think they needed to teach me how to write. Editors have even said things like, 'Send me a *good* story next time.' I've tried to extract the most valuable information from critiques like that—such as specific tips on writing for that editor's magazine—without getting depressed by the way the criticism was given. I know it's only one person's opinion. An editor may even criticize your work while using an in-house writer whose work is inferior to yours. I accept the fact that, as a freelancer, I'm in competition with staff writers—we're the lowest-ranking people editors deal with because we're outsiders. So I don't take anything about my work for granted.

"You must have confidence in yourself! You must be persistent and relentless! Freelance magazine writing is like going to war. You have a mission—to get published—and don't bother coming back unless you're victorious! But I enjoy what I do so much that I see it in the most positive light. I love film, and as a writer you have to care about your subject. It's hard to do good work otherwise, although I *have* been assigned a profile, say, of a director whose work I'm not especially fond of and been pleasantly surprised. I enjoy discovering something about film or a filmmaker or an actor that I didn't know before. I've learned to get to know people I would have wrongly given up on.

"As a freelance writer you've got to have a thick skin. You're not always going to be treated very nicely, and you've got to be prepared and not take it to heart. After all, it's your life. How can you let your life be affected by other people's opinions or moods?"

{ 8 }

STICKY SITUATIONS—
AND HOW TO GET OUT OF THEM

Uh-oh. You've got a problem with an editor. It may or may not be a situation *you* created, but you need some answers—fast.

Here's an assortment of typical magazine-related dilemmas, one or more you may have already encountered as a freelancer, as well as savvy ways to solve them.

1. "EDITORS IGNORE ME!"

When editors pay no attention to you, the first thing you've got to do is determine exactly what's going on. Think about it. Might they be *deliberately* shunning you because you've been making a pest of yourself with incessant phone calls and letters? Cool it for awhile, then try again in a month or two, exercising greater restraint than you did the last time.

Perhaps you've struck out with your last couple of assignments at a given magazine and the editors are reluctant to take a chance with you again. If you're hell-bent on continuing to write for them, take some time to figure out how and why your stories missed the boat. Really *study* current issues to see what their published freelancers are doing right in terms of ideas, research, and writing style. Then try again.

It *may* simply be that the magazine you're anxious to break into is terrible about getting back to writers (especially ones they don't know). If you feel you're getting the runaround because of staff incompetence—for example, your query keeps getting bounced from one editor's desk to another but no one ever responds—move on. This scenario does not bode well for future dealings with the magazine, and there are plenty of others that will be glad to consider your ideas and work with you.

2. "MY FRIEND AND I WRITE FOR THE SAME MAGAZINE, BUT SHE GETS PAID MORE THAN I DO!"

It is frustrating to discover that a magazine is paying a friend of yours more than it pays you, but don't panic. Consider the obvious possibilities. Her pieces may be longer or more complicated or both. She may be writing for the "well" (the middle part of the magazine, where the longer features generally appear), while you're writing for the front-of-the-book, where pieces traditionally pay less. Perhaps she's worked for the magazine longer than you have and has received one or more "raises" over time.

If you don't come up with any solid reasons why her pieces earn more, look at the situation as a plus: It means the magazine can be bargained with. Without naming names, let your editor know that you're aware that "certain freelancers" are earning more for comparable articles, and suggest it may be time for a raise. And of course, if *Writer's Market* or a similar magazine directory indicates that this publication usually pays more than you're receiving, mention that fact immediately. (By the way, how did you let *that* happen?)

3. "THE MAGAZINE REWROTE MY PIECE—AND IT'S AWFUL!"

There's nothing more upsetting than seeing your name on an article that bears little resemblance to the one you submitted. The majority of reputable magazines do not make significant changes in a piece without showing the author galleys. However, just about every freelance writer has at least one horror story involving phantom leads, paragraphs and even *quotes* that somehow found their way into their published articles.

Should this happen to you, you're wise (and certainly within your rights) to speak up to your assigning editor and let her know how unhappy you are, especially if you intend to continue working with this publication. Get her assurance that no changes will be made in your manuscripts in the future without your approval, and insist on always seeing first, second, and even third galleys.

But many freelancers would just as soon kiss off magazines that are this cavalier about the way they deal with articles—and writers. If you can afford to walk, you should—otherwise your reputation as a writer may suffer.

Something else to keep in mind: Certain magazines assume that they're buying *research* from freelancers, and their articles are blatantly and unapologetically rewritten in-house. Again, you have the option of voting with your feet should you find yourself dealing with such a magazine.

4. "THE MAGAZINE THAT BOUGHT MY ARTICLE FOLDED!"

If you are ever unfortunate enough to work for a magazine that goes out of business, let's hope you got paid before it folded. Whether or not you did, the rights to your unpublished story automatically revert back to you, and you're free to resell it somewhere else. If you *didn't* receive payment and you're the type who doesn't mind spending your days drafting nasty letters and hanging around a courthouse, you can try suing the company in Small Claims Court. (If you're a member of a writers' organization, you'll have even more clout than if you attempt to sue on your own.)

5. "IT TAKES FOREVER TO GET PAID!"

There's no reason why it should take more than a month or two after your piece has been accepted to receive payment. Phone your assigning editor and nicely ask him to put pressure on the accounting department. If possible, see if he can give you a date when you can expect your money. Wait the allotted number of days. No luck? Call again, this time asking if he'd mind your contacting the accounting people yourself. (He probably won't and might actually welcome your taking over this onerous task.) Continue your polite-but-firm weekly calls to the editor and the accounting department. Sooner or later you'll see your money. (This wearisome procedure is one reason why it pays to diversify and *not* count on any one or two magazines for your income.)

6. "MY ARTICLE IDEA WAS TURNED DOWN, ONLY TO APPEAR IN THE MAGAZINE FOUR MONTHS LATER UNDER SOMEONE ELSE'S BYLINE!"

Many beginning writers are terrified that their story ideas will get ripped off, but editors don't need to do that. That's not to say it *never* happens, but it happens a lot less frequently than novice writers think. So when you see "your" recently rejected article idea in the very same magazine you queried, chances are the editors (or one of their regular freelancers) thought of it long before you did.

7. "I'VE JUST BEEN GIVEN AN ASSIGNMENT I DON'T REALLY WANT TO DO!"

Sooner or later every writer is faced with an assignment that is difficult to like. Well, let's analyze this a minute. Is it a case where you want to develop a relationship with the editor, the magazine came up with the idea, and it's your first assignment? Even if you don't love the topic, bite the bullet and do it! And while you're at it, do such a terrific job that the editor will be glad to entertain *your* story ideas the next time around.

Is it a situation where you said yes because you don't know *how* to say no? Some writers automatically accept every assignment they're offered because they're grateful and afraid they'll never be asked again. This may be true if an editor doesn't know you, but once you're past that stage you have a lot more leeway.

So let's assume you already have something of a relationship with this assigning editor. If you've said yes when you really wanted to say no because you don't have the interest, time, or energy to write this particular piece— *and* you feel confident it won't greatly inconvenience your editor—ask nicely to be let off the hook. Thank the editor for the assignment, explain the situation, apologize for accepting it too readily, and immediately ask if you can try something else. Most editors won't have a problem with this at all. (And next time around, think before you speak.)

8. "NO ONE WILL TELL ME THE STATUS OF THE PIECE I WROTE ON ASSIGNMENT—AND IT'S BEEN TWO MONTHS!"

It's maddening to be given an assignment, work your head off doing a good job, and then have to wait weeks and even months to hear if it's been okayed. This can occur because several editors must approve the piece, because the staff is inept, or because your assigning editor got fired and nobody bothered to inform you. But *you* also have a responsibility to stay on top of the situation. So don't wait more than a week or two after submitting your piece to find out if it's been accepted or at least read. Don't hang up until you get an approximate date when you can expect to hear back from your editor. Make weekly phone calls to that editor until you know what's going on and when you can expect to see payment and publication of the story.

In extreme cases, you may hear nothing concrete for *months,* despite all your efforts. You should then write a letter to your assigning editor, carbon-copying the editor-in-chief, recapping all that's been going on, and indicating that if the piece is not being used, you expect a prompt kill-fee payment. Indicate that you are officially withdrawing the piece from the magazine; you can then feel free to try to sell it elsewhere.

} 9 {

EARNING A LIVING
FROM YOUR WRITING

Norman Schreiber, a successful freelance writer, says that it wasn't until he had been writing for many years that he had his consciousness raised about the magazine-publishing business. "For a long time," he now admits, "my idea of negotiation was saying 'Thank you very much.'"

As Norman has come to understand (and it is hoped you will too), there's more to earning decent money as a writer than simply accepting what's offered. The first step is getting out of the habit of acting as though an editor is doing you a favor by giving you an assignment. It's an attitude widespread among beginning writers and a difficult one to change—but you can, and indeed *must*, if you're ever to become serious about your work. Realize that magazine publishing is a business like any other; no editor is going to lay out the publisher's dough unless you can give the magazine what it wants.

Below are additional suggestions for turning your writing hobby into a business and beginning to make real money from it:

1. ALWAYS WRITE ON ASSIGNMENT

The difference between amateurs and pros is that pros don't spend their time drafting a proposal, doing research, conducting interviews, transcribing notes, and writing, rewriting, and editing their manuscript unless they have a pretty good idea someone will eventually *buy* it. That's altogether too much work to do for nothing. Except in the very, very early stages of your career, when you need the clips more than you need the cash, never work on speculation. Insist on an assignment and a kill-fee agreement. The more you treat your work as though it's worthy of decent payment, the more decent payment it will get.

And if it doesn't come naturally, learn to *act* insulted if someone asks about a piece you're writing, "Is this an assignment?"

2. USE THE ONE-HUNDRED-DOLLARS-MORE RULE

Freelance writer April Koral lives by what she calls her one-hundred-dollars-more rule: Ask for an additional hundred dollars (or more if you feel comfortable about it) whenever an editor quotes you a dollar figure for an assignment. Alternatively, you could say something like, "I'm going to have to do a lot of work on this article . . . can you do any better?" You shouldn't try this all the time, but every now and then is fine. Of course, there's no guarantee you'll get what you ask for, but there *is* a good chance she'll kick in a few extra bucks, especially if she's fond of you (and knows you've been underpaid all along).

Needless to say, be sure all your relevant expenses—long-distance calls, transportation, and so on—are being picked up by the magazine.

3. GET FRIENDLY WITH THE ACCOUNTING DEPARTMENT

To assure speedy payment, it's a good idea to make contact with the accounting department. I don't mean *hound* them. But the first time there's a delay with a check, give them a call and let them know, in a pleasant way, who you are—and then ask if there's anything you can do to help speed things along. Call the accounting folks by name. (A good tip with anyone with whom you work.) If at all possible, pick up your check in person at least once so they can match the name with the face.

It has always seemed to me as an editor that my most promptly paid freelance writers were the ones who knew how to shmooze the accounting people. If you feel comfortable doing it and it doesn't seem phony, do it.

4. BE CAREFUL OF THE RIGHTS YOU SIGN AWAY

In 1989 the Supreme Court ruled that writers and other artists retain the right to copyright their work so long as they are not in an "employee relationship" with the editor or publisher who seeks their work. This means your rights as a writer are protected more than ever before. Now it's harder for a magazine to impose a "work-for-hire" rule, which would permit that company to "hire" you to write an article and then own it.

"Work-for-hire" agreements and the publications that insist upon them are rapidly disappearing (although one or two major magazine companies, such as the Des Moines–based Meredith Corporation, which publishes *Better Homes and Gardens,* still insist on them). You will find that usually the magazine is offering to pay you for only one-time use of your article—it does not have the right to reprint or otherwise use your material again without paying you an additional fee.

While most beginning writers are grateful for *any* assignments they get, professional writers know it's crucial to retain as many rights as possible to their work—otherwise thousands of dollars in reprint and syndication sales could be lost.

The bottom line is: Read your contracts carefully to see exactly what you're agreeing to. If there's any negotiating to be done, do it *before* you sign.

5. SHIFT FROM LOW-PAYING MARKETS TO HIGH-PAYING ONES

Remember the old adage, "It's just as easy to fall in love with a rich man as it is with a poor one"? Well, it's not so different when it comes to magazine writing. Sure, it's harder to get a gig as a contributing writer to *Vanity Fair* (several of whom have $100,000-a-year contracts) than it is to work for *Trailer Life,* which pays around $250 for its articles. But there's a lot of middle ground. You'll find, for example, that some travel magazines pay ten cents a word while others pay a dollar a word. Why start at the bottom when you can start at the top?

If you're going to compile a list of possible magazines for your article idea, submit *first* to the best and highest-paying ones. Believe in yourself and in your abilities. Act as though you deserve to write for the best magazines in the world and soon you will be.

6. SET FINANCIAL GOALS FOR YOURSELF—AND MEET THEM

I've always found it challenging—and rewarding—to start the new year with a set of financial goals for my free-lance writing. I determine how much money I think I'll need for the year, my various sources of income (for example, my steady editing job, regular columns, book sales, miscellaneous articles, foreign and reprint sales), and how much or little I'll have to put into each area to achieve my goals.

There have been terrific years when I've pretty much met my goal by October and didn't need to drum up any additional freelance work until January; other years I've missed my goal by several thousand dollars. But just as I'd never dream of accepting a full-time job without knowing the annual salary it pays, I couldn't have a career as a freelance writer without having a reasonable sense of what I'll be earning from one year to the next—and how much work it will take to get it.

7. PAY ATTENTION TO THE NEW TAX LAWS AND HOW THEY AFFECT YOU

The tax laws have recently been revised, and these changes affect, among others, freelance writers. Tax expert Julian Block offers the following useful tips. An attorney in

Larchmont, New York, he is the author of *Julian Block's Year-round Tax Strategies for the $40,000+ Household* (Prima Publishing).

1. Business entertainment costs, which might be a meal or drinks, are not fully tax deductible, as they were prior to the 1986 tax revision; they are now only 80 percent deductible. As a result, you'll have to subtract 20 percent of those expenses from your Schedule C before you claim them. (The Schedule C of the 1040 form is the one on which freelancers list their receipts and subtract their expenses to determine their net profit.)

2. If you use part of your home as an office, you'll have to be very careful about justifying the expenses you claim for rent and utilities (including phone), particularly since the IRS has tightened the rules concerning home offices. To qualify for an office-at-home deduction, you need to set aside a portion of your residence to be used *exclusively* and *regularly* for your writing. It doesn't have to be a separate room, but it should be a separate area not used for any other purpose. There are two IRS-approved ways to compute the deduction: multiply your total office-at-home expenses by either (1) the percentage of the total number of rooms in the house used as an office or (2) the percentage of total floor area of the house used as an office—whichever gives you the bigger deduction.

3. Maintain detailed and accurate records of your expenses. Keep all receipts related to your writing, and don't overlook some less-obvious expenses you may incur—for example, videocassette rentals and *TV Guide* subscriptions if you're an entertainment writer, business-seminar costs if you're a financial writer. *Get and keep receipts for everything,* from PCs to paper clips.

4. If you earn all or most of your income as a freelancer, you will generally have to pay federal and state taxes quarterly (January, April, June, September), rather than annually. After you or your accountant (or both of you) have come up with rough estimates for what you'll owe each quarter, plan accordingly. For example, some writers put the earnings from one or more articles they've written directly into a separate fund earmarked to pay taxes.

5. Certain extraordinary requirements for your home office may enable you to take additional deductions. For instance, if your word processor needs to be in a very cool environment, you may incur higher air-conditioning bills, or if you live in an old house, your writing equipment may require additional wiring. These higher business-related expenses would be deductible.

6. Be scrupulous about your phone expenses, and be sure to keep your personal and business calls and faxes separate. If you don't have a separate phone for your writing business, at least be certain that you can clearly demonstrate which calls are directly related to your work. The best way to keep track? Keep a log of all your business calls.

7. If you utilize the services of someone to help you with your writing business—typist, secretary or gofer, researcher, lawyer, accountant, consultant—those fees are generally 100 percent deductible, but check the deduction rules.

8. As a self-employed person, you'll need to provide yourself and your family with some financial security. One of the best ways is by setting up a Self-Employment Pension plan (SEP) or Keogh. Talk to your accountant about the advantages and disadvantages of each to decide which is

better for you. Either one will enable you to salt away money for your retirement while reducing your current tax bill and deferring interest or other earnings on the accrued savings. If you're just starting out, you probably won't be able to put aside immediately the maximum allowed, but do have a financial plan you can stick with.

9. Try to *earn* more from your writing than you *spend* in writing-related expenses. Otherwise, the IRS folks may contend that what you call a business venture is actually a hobby—and hobby expenses are *not* deductible.

8. JOIN A PROFESSIONAL WRITERS' GROUP

I'm a member of both the American Society of Journalists and Authors and the National Writers Union. I've found that attending meetings where I am surrounded by accomplished, successful freelancers and can swap inside information about magazines and editors has been good for inspiration—and my wallet. These organizations also publish valuable newsletters that provide leads and tips not found anywhere else. No question: I've made money and important contacts as a result of being a part of these groups. As soon as you qualify for membership in a professional writers' organization, join.

9. DETERMINE IF YOU'VE GOT WHAT IT TAKES

Can you make it financially as a writer? Here are some questions to ask yourself:

174

- How successful and disciplined have you been thus far?
- Are your assignments growing increasingly profitable and prestigious?
- Have you (more or less) met the financial goals you've set for yourself?
- Have your writing contacts expanded? Is it generally easier to get work? Do editors occasionally call *you* to give you assignments?
- How many mouths do you have to feed—and do they prefer Chicken McNuggets or *canard à l'orange*?
- Do you find the writer's life dreamy—or drudgery?

While the flexibility, creativity, and fun of a freelance-writing career may sound great, most people, if truth be told, find it a very difficult way of life unless they (1) only do it part-time; (2) have a steady gig or two, such as writing regular columns; or (3) are part of a two- (or more) income family. There is nothing more hellish than living from check to check. Even if you're one of those writers who is constantly bubbling over with story ideas (and such folks are rare), you cannot control when (or if) your article will be assigned, read, approved, and paid for. It's hard to be creative when you're worried—and worry becomes a way of life for many freelancers who don't provide themselves with a sufficient financial cushion.

Writing, although a wonderfully satisfying career for many, has enough negative about it (much of which has already been discussed in these pages) to give would-be freelancers pause. Prepare yourself wisely before you take the plunge. And if it doesn't work out, there are plenty of other jobs out there—the vast majority of which will pay for your health insurance.

} 10 {

FINAL WORDS

1. FORGET ABOUT PERFECTIONISM

Too many freelance writers wait—feverishly working and reworking their copy—until their article is "perfect" before submitting it to a magazine. *No* article is perfect; each one can be improved upon in some way. Yet being imperfect doesn't mean it's not *salable.* If you want a career as a writer you've got to be realistic about how much time and energy you can afford to put into your work. So, submit *the best work you can do; then get on with it.*

If you're having trouble with this concept, ask yourself, What's the worst that can happen? The article you're so pleased with gets rejected. (And *that* probably won't happen until you've been given at least one crack at fixing it and making it acceptable to the editor.) So *what?* It's a disappointment, but who *hasn't* gotten rejected in life? At least you'll get a kill fee if this was an assigned article. Your next job is to find another magazine for which your story might be suited. Whip up another copy of your original query letter (making all the appropriate changes, of course) and send it off to another publication. No magazine is unique. The typical piece could conceivably be bought by a fair number of magazines *without a single revision.* (With revision, that number increases.)

Who knows? Your piece might just be picked up by the second magazine. Then your combined earnings from your kill fee and the payment from the sale to the second magazine might add up to more than you'd originally expected. And it will help you get over the feeling that you're not a publishable writer.

2. DO YOUR BEST; DON'T WORRY ABOUT BEING THE BEST

What's the best, anyway? Is "The Cosby Show" the best sitcom on television? Popular as it is, Roseanne Barr came along and stole a lot of attention away from old Bill. There's room on TV—and in the movies, in the bookstores, in magazines, everywhere—for plenty of *good.* If your fear of not being the best is paralyzing you and keeping you from progressing in your writing, remind yourself that not everything you see, hear, read, or eat is necessarily the best of its kind but *is* good enough to earn the appreciation of *someone.* Which leads to . . .

3. REMEMBER IT ONLY TAKES ONE YES TO SELL AN ARTICLE

Let's say you were in the market for a spouse. For whatever reason, you believe you'll have a hard time of it. But the reality is you have approximately half the world of the opposite sex at your disposal. Even after weeding out the ones who don't quite strike your fancy, you *still* have a tremendous number to choose from—and it only takes one to say "Will you marry me?" to get the wedding plans in motion.

The same basic principle is true when it comes to selling a magazine piece. Maybe you've never done it before. You're not quite sure which magazine is right for your idea. You think the odds are against you. But there are *thousands* of publications out there—and it only takes *one* for you to make the transition from unpublished to published writer. And the more that say yes, the easier it gets to make future sales.

4. STRIKE A BALANCE BETWEEN DOING QUALITY WORK AND EARNING MONEY

The most successful—and happy—freelance writers I know are ones who are concerned with the quality of the work they produce *as well as* with the income they produce. It's those who focus too much on quality or earnings *at the expense of the other* who run into trouble.

If you're spending too many days or weeks on your golden prose, your output will suffer—and so will your bank account. You'll probably never earn enough money from your writing to be able to support yourself—at least not without a trust fund or an understanding mate. On the other hand, if you're sitting midarticle at the computer and you're already calculating the money you'll make from the original sale, foreign and domestic reprint sales, and miniseries rights, chances are you're not working hard enough at the *writing*.

You've got to have pride in your work. If you're sincere

about building a career as a freelancer, you've got to really care about your writing. But *don't* care to the point where you can only manage to complete two five-hundred-dollar stories a year. Find a comfortable balance for yourself, where you can be satisfied with your writing and with the income it generates. When that delicate balance is struck, your motivation to *keep* writing will be that much greater.

5. DON'T GET DISCOURAGED

Once you decide you're going to try to make it as a free-lancer—whatever "make it" means to you—you'll be leaving yourself open to subtle and not-so-subtle rejection. The negativity you'll encounter will range from people wondering when you're going to get a *real* job to opening an envelope from *GQ* (with your name misspelled) containing a form rejection slip. Rejection is a way of life for freelancers even after getting published.

My mother (God bless her, as they always say at this juncture) is a wonderful woman. What's more, she's always been a compulsive reader of books and magazines. Yet like most mothers she didn't want to see her children struggle any more than necessary. So she didn't encourage my writing ambitions, which first emerged around the time I was in kindergarten. My poems and stories were, if truth be told, astounding for a five-year-old. Maybe Mom knew it, maybe she didn't, but she had visions of me living in an empty refrigerator carton if I were foolish enough to pursue a writing career. So very early on she began trying to convince me to be a teacher. (Yup, here's another one of those you-can-always-fall-back-on-your-teaching stories.)

Unfortunately, I listened to her and spent two of the most dreadful years of my life as an employee of the New

York City public-school system. I was no Miss Brooks; kids and I just didn't mix. It was a toss-up who was happiest to see me leave P.S. 122—the students, the principal, or I.

I also remember my college journalism teacher, who only gave me a *B* on an essay I wrote about love and who told me during a student-teacher conference that he felt I had no real gift for writing. As it turned out, the grade-*B* essay was published on the Op-Ed page of *The New York Times,* and I'm certain I'm earning more today as a writer than he is as a college teacher.

So here I am, two decades later, enjoying my life as a freelance writer and editor. I temporarily believed the negative comments about my potential and I temporarily went astray, but I guess I always believed I could succeed at what I'm doing—and loving—now.

Freelance writing is not for the faint of heart. If you're easily hurt and take rejection personally, believe me, there are *lots* of simpler ways to earn a living. But if you pride yourself on being self-confident and take most rejection in stride, forge ahead.

6. MAKE SURE IT'S MAKING YOU HAPPY

Life is short. If you find that being a freelance writer is keeping you angry, anxious, frustrated, or poor, do something else. Work takes up the greatest portion of your waking time; it should bring you pleasure.

GLOSSARY

Byline: The line containing the name of the author of an article. The line usually appears near the title of the article but may be found at the end if the article is very brief or is a **sidebar** to a larger story.
Example: "I'm glad I saw the galleys of my article—my name had been misspelled in the byline!"

Clips: Originals or photocopies of a writer's published articles. They are often requested by an editor before assigning an article to a writer new to that magazine.
Example: "I always include one or two clips of my best articles when querying a magazine for the first time."

Coverlines: Eye-catching article titles and topics listed on the cover of a magazine in the hopes of "selling" that issue.
Example: "*Baked Goods Weekly* used my article 'White, Rye or Pumpernickel: What Your Bread Preferences Say About You' as a coverline on their August 27th issue."

First North American rights: The right of a magazine buying an article to publish it for the first time anywhere in North America. Afterward all other publication rights revert back to the writer.
Example: "I only sell first North American rights so I can try to resell my piece to other magazines."

Front-of-the-book: The front section of a magazine, which traditionally contains shorter pieces, regular columns, mini-features, newsbreaks, and so on. These pieces generally pay less than **well** articles.
Example: "I'd like to move away from doing front-of-the-book stories. How about a bigger assignment?"

Hook: A twist or an angle, ideally one that makes an idea for an article interesting and fresh, usually helped by a clever title.
Example: "I just sold a piece on women's obsession with tanning. I gave it an unusual hook and called it 'Tanorexia.'"

Kill fee: The reduced payment given a writer when an assigned article is not used, usually amounting to 20 or 25 percent of the originally agreed-upon payment.
Example: "You pay only a 15 percent kill fee? Given all the work I've done, is there any possibility you could bring it up to 20 percent?"

Lead time: The length of time between the editing of a particular article and its appearance in the magazine. Most monthly magazines have three- to four-month lead times.
Example: "I submitted my Halloween feature in June because I knew the magazine had a four-month lead time."

Line editing: The fine-tuning an editor gives an article to make it clearer and stronger. This may include alterations in spelling, punctuation, grammar, structure, and wording. *Example:* "My editor at *Glamour* always sends me galleys of my articles so I can okay her line-editing changes."

Masthead: The list of editors, along with their titles, found near the front of a magazine. *Example:* "Would you consider listing me as a contributing editor on the masthead?"

Multiple submission: An original article or query submitted to two or more magazines at the same time (a practice frowned upon by most editors). *Example:* "Because it may take editors weeks or months to respond to my ideas, I occasionally do a multiple submission to save time."

On assignment: With a commission from a magazine to write a piece, which the magazine fully expects to buy and publish. If the magazine does not buy the assigned article for any reason, it agrees to pay a **kill fee.** *Example:* "You're offering me $750 for this article on assignment? Any chance of getting it up to $1000?"

On spec: On speculation, without guarantee of use or payment. *Example:* "First pieces for your magazine are always on spec? Well, as a professional, I only work on assignment."

On the record/Off the record: Whether or not the quotes given to the writer may be used for attribution in a story. *Example:* "Of course I'll respect your wish to keep your comments off the record."

One-time use: The right of a magazine to publish an article only once. Should the magazine wish to use it in one of its sister publications or for promotional purposes, it must pay the writer an additional fee.

Example: "I sold *Woman Today* one-time-use rights to my article, and I then received an extra ten percent when part of the article was reprinted in an advertising mailing piece."

Over the transom: Unsolicited. (See **Slush pile.**)

Example: "Because editors rarely buy over-the-transom manuscripts, I always send query letters first."

Pitch letter: The proposal a writer sends an editor in the hopes of getting an article assignment; also called a **query letter.**

Example: "The editor loved my pitch letter on Leona Helmsley and gave me a $750 assignment."

Press junket: A sponsored trip, usually paid for by a government tourist office, airline, hotel, and so on. Professional travel writers are invited on junkets in the hopes they will write and publish favorable articles about the destination.

Example: "I've discovered that more and more travel publications refuse to accept articles based on press junkets."

Query letter: See **Pitch letter.**

SASE: "Self-addressed stamped envelope."

Example: "I no longer send an SASE with my query or manuscript. Like most professional writers, I let the magazine pay my return-postage cost."

Sidebar: A mini-article or "box" accompanying a longer article, dealing with a related subject.
Example: "After my piece on headaches was accepted, I was asked to write a sidebar listing headache clinics around the country."

Slush pile: The "pile" of manuscripts that come in to a magazine over the transom. Slush-pile submissions are not considered high-priority reading.
Example: "My assigned article wound up in the *Bunny Monthly* slush pile, and it took the editor two years to get to it!"

Stringer: A writer who works part-time for a newspaper or magazine and is usually based in a major city outside that publication's headquarters.
Example: "Benedict Nightingale is a London-based theater stringer for *The New York Times.*"

Tearsheets: Pages that carry your article, torn or clipped from a magazine.
Example: "Could you possibly send me a tearsheet of my story in the April issue?"

TK: "To come"; used in place of the information missing from your article.
Example: "I always make sure I fill in all my TKs before submitting articles to my editors."

Well: Generally speaking, the middle section of a magazine, where the major features begin. These are usually the most important and best-paid pieces.
Example: "How much do you pay for a 'well' story of about 2,000 words?"

Work-for-hire agreement: An agreement whereby a publisher "hires" a writer to do an article and then owns all rights to it.

Example: "As a professional writer I never sign work-for-hire agreements, only one-time-use contracts."